Leadership

FOR

LAWYERS

Second Edition

Leadership
FOR
LAWYERS

Second Edition

HERB RUBINSTEIN

AMERICAN BAR ASSOCIATION
Defending Liberty
Pursuing Justice

Cover design by ABA Publishing

11 10 09 08 07   5 4 3 2 1

Cataloging-in-Publication data is on file with the Library of Congress

Leadership for lawyers / Herb Rubenstein

Discounts are available for books ordered in bulk. Special consideration is given to state bars, CLE programs, and other bar-related organizations. Inquire at Book Publishing, ABA Publishing, American Bar Association, 321 North Clark Street, Chicago, Illinois 60610.

www.ababooks.org

Contents

Introduction

Leadership has become a popular subject in the past several years. All one needs to do is peruse the management section in any bookstore to confirm that fact. In fact, one might argue that "leadership" has become an essential skill in this century's first decade. The proliferation of leadership books and articles might have the unintended consequence of convincing some lawyers that leadership is merely the latest fad, soon to be replaced by another "flavor of the month" in the annals of management literature.

Drawing such a conclusion would not only be foolish but dangerous for the future of legal organizations. Every legal organization, large or small, needs excellent leadership. Our clients need it. All organizations benefit from wise, enlightened, and visionary leadership.

Unfortunately, most lawyers have not benefited from a formal education in leadership. Leadership is not taught in law school to any significant extent. It is only now becoming the subject of a few select CLE courses. The majority of lawyers in the legal profession have developed what leadership skills they have the hard way: through experience, through mistakes, and, if they are fortunate, from mentors with years of leadership experience. But few law firms have any mentoring program at all that formally links new associates and junior partners with senior partners who could impart some leadership development education.

My interest in the leadership field grew from my first exposure to Stephen Covey's *The Seven Habits of Highly Effective People,* now the best-selling business book ever published. After reading that book, I decided to become a licensed facilitator of the workshop based upon it. For the past eight years, I have facilitated these workshops for employees at my parent institution, Georgetown University, and have delivered many lectures and workshops based on this material for organizations and associations across the United States.

This, in turn, produced a greater interest in the entire field of leadership, and as I immersed myself in the readings of leadership pioneers from Robert Greenleaf to Warren Bennis to Peter Senge, I began to wonder why this leadership revolution has not made its way into my profession, the legal profession.

For the past 25 years, I have been involved in the continuing legal education industry. Since 1985, I have served as the head of a continuing legal education department at Georgetown University Law Center in Washington, D.C. During these past 20 years, I have served as a leader and active member of the Association for Continuing Legal Education, the international organization representing the CLE industry. As a part of my job during this span of more than two decades, I have followed closely the trends within the legal profession.

The practice of law in 2007 is far different than it was 20 years ago. The collegiality that characterized law firms of the 1980s is missing from many law firms today. The emphasis on the bottom line has dramatically increased. Whereas law firms used to wait for clients to walk through the front door or depend on several big rainmakers, today more and more law firms are hiring chief marketing officers. Some firms are even training their lawyers in sales skills, once a foreign word for law firms. Firms are also hiring chief operating officers or chief business officers, adopting the corporate model utilized by many of their brethren in the private sector.

One would think that in this era of emphasis on the bottom line, on business practices and on client development, small and large law firms, general counsel offices, government agencies that hire lawyers, nonprofit organizations with legal staffs, all would have embraced leadership development as an essential tool for today's lawyers. After all, excellent leadership would help a legal organization become more efficient, attract more clients, work together more effectively, retain its top lawyers and staff members, and be more successful. Nevertheless, a large majority of our legal organizations have not devoted dollars and time to teaching their managing partners, practice group heads, senior partners, and senior associates or leaders about leadership. Solo practitioners, who are called upon every day to help lead community organizations, have not yet flocked to take a leadership development course. Why, in this decade of rapid change in the legal profession, when corporations, MBA programs, and other professions are devoting so many resources to leadership training, have legal organizations, including law firms, dragged their feet on leadership development?

Traditionally, corporations have been years ahead of law firms in adopting training techniques and mandating training for all employees. Whether one considers the benefits of distance learning or the widespread adoption of on-line education, corporations have been training employees around the world for many years. Only recently have law firms and other legal organizations begun considering and implementing such programs.

Law firms have eschewed training in what many consider "soft skills" for decades. Traditional continuing legal education has focused upon substantive law developments or the improvement of identified legal skills. Continuing legal education providers who have offered courses in management or leadership skills for lawyers have encountered difficulties in getting these courses accredited for Mandatory Continuing Legal Education credit or have seen these courses suffer from very low attendance. Even in-house training courses in management and leadership have been rare.

The lack of these courses is ironic because leaders in legal organizations are generally smart, with years of formal education and years of experience in the workplace. Intellectually, they know that a successful law firm or legal organization must be supported and led by great leadership. They know that such leadership must include a commitment to hiring the right people, lawyers and non-lawyers, putting them in the proper jobs, and then "growing" these people as they progress through their careers.

Leaders in the legal profession who wish to grow their employees and serve their clients more successfully have to start with a solid knowledge of what it takes to be a successful leader. This requires understanding leadership theory and practice. Leaders must understand the ethics of leadership and the role it must play every day in how they interact with adversaries, clients, vendors, employees, judges, and the myriad of people we work with every day in the legal profession. Leadership means holding people accountable and not settling for anything less than the best. In order to be leaders who create other leaders, they must stretch their employees and put them in uncomfortable positions—positions that require them to face new problems and develop new solutions. They must persuade their people that they can establish ambitious goals and meet them and that they have exciting professional futures.

Too often, law firms and legal organizations focus only on people's professional lives. Yet if they are to truly coach people and develop leaders, they must pay attention to their personal lives as well. They must focus on their competence and their character, making sincere investments of time in their people. Getting to know colleagues as people and not just as workers can pay huge dividends for leaders in legal organizations. If people know that their leaders care for them as human beings, are respectful of their strengths and weaknesses, and are always striving to put them in the best possible light in front of their peers and others, they will be willing to go the extra mile when it becomes necessary. And when they become leaders later in their careers, they will demonstrate the same behavior with their peers and colleagues.

Excellent leaders at law firms and legal organizations know what motivates their people. Like a coach or manager of a sports team, they must balance egos and needs. They must know who is motivated by a pat on the back and who is motivated by a push. At the same time they motivate people, great legal leaders encourage lawyers and non-lawyers to develop their skills—skills that further their career aspirations while serving the firm. Simultaneously, they help people develop knowledge about their jobs, about their clients, about the firm, and about the role they play at the firm.

Great leaders do not stop at helping people identify the skills and knowledge they wish to gain. They also assist them in identifying the relationships they need to build. They realize that effective human relationships are the underpinning of every employee's—lawyers and non-lawyers—professional success. Great leaders know that they must lead and develop other people. To do so, they must serve as role models. As role models, they know that people pay much more attention to what they do than what they say. Lawyers have an enormous impact upon the people they serve, and for this reason alone, leadership development books and training designed specifically for lawyers and those in the legal profession can pay huge dividends.

The important process of our law profession investing more diligently in leadership development will not occur overnight. It will take place gradually, one step at a time. Legal organizations' leaders must be educated about leadership principles, about the evolution of leadership knowledge in this country and its value for organizations. They must see the positive effect of leadership training at peer law firms and within legal agencies. Slowly this process is starting to take place. Several years ago, the national law firm Reed Smith, LLP started Reed Smith University in conjunction with the Wharton School of Business. A significant part of the curriculum is leadership. Also, the international law firm DLA Piper Rudnick, LLP signed a contract with the Harvard Business School to teach leadership and management skills to its firm leaders.

Much more is needed. A paradigm shift must take place. Fortunately, books like this one will help lead the way. In this important work, Herb Rubenstein shows lawyers why leadership is so vital for every successful law firm in the 21st century. He takes the reader on a guided tour of the leadership literature of the past 50 years. He identifies the various brands of leadership that authors and businessmen have been teaching and practicing, pointing out the strengths and weaknesses of each. He shares success stories of leaders who have practiced leadership skills in order to lead their firms and companies to new heights. Finally, Herb introduces the reader to the critical concept of "leaders of leaders," people who can significantly impact the legal profession for decades to come.

I invite you to take this leadership journey with Herb as your guide. It will enlighten you, educate you, and inspire you. Most important, it will change you.

Lawrence J. Center
Georgetown University Law Center

Author's Preface to the Second Edition

Much has happened over the past five years regarding leadership development in the legal profession. There are new leadership courses for lawyers and professionals at all levels in our profession. There is a greater interest by law firms and lawyers in studying leadership, and there is a growing awareness of the positive impact leadership development can play in our profession.

In addition, bar associations, CLE providers, and the federal government have all begun to invest in this new and growing educational opportunity that is having a positive impact on the legal profession. The American Bar Association, in spearheading the publication of this second edition, has expanded its already broad commitment to the legal profession to include making a substantial investment in helping lawyers become better leaders.

This edition includes several new chapters and discusses several new players in the legal profession who have gone on record calling for law schools to teach leadership and for lawyers to begin to improve their leadership skills. Law students have begun to express a strong interest in improving their leadership skills. Bob Cullen has created a course on leadership for law students at Santa Clara Law School, and Phil Heymann continues to teach his course on leadership at Harvard Law School. George Gilbert, currently a student of the Georgetown University Law Center, my alma mater, worked on the first edition of the book and, in his separate preface to this edition, explains why this book is so valuable for law students.

The Wisconsin Bar Association has leadership courses where over 15 hours of CLE credit has been approved. In Colorado, Gary Abrams, director of CLE for the Colorado Bar Association, is planning a series of leadership courses both in a stand-up format and in "webinars."

For an author who wrote the first book on leadership for lawyers, this is gratifying. This second edition improves on the first edition in four significant ways. First, we include developments in the field over the past two years since the first edition was published by the National Institute for Trial Advocacy. Second, we provide a chapter on leadership assessment and show that these leadership assessment tools can be very beneficial to individual lawyers seeking to become better leaders, and law firms that want to cultivate better leadership among their partners and associates. Third, we have completely rewritten our chapter on women in the legal profession. Women still face huge challenges and barriers to becoming leaders on a larger scale in our profession. We discuss those challenges and identify how in the past two years women have been making significant progress in obtaining leadership positions in the legal profession. Fourth, we have created a road map for lawyers, law firms, and legal organizations to follow if they want to offer leadership development programs and courses to their partners and employees.

Lawyers are called upon to be leaders every day in their professional lives. Yet, most of us have no formal training in the area of leadership development, and courses on leadership are still not available in every state. This book represents only a small step toward helping those in our profession become better leaders. This book has many audiences:

- individual lawyers,
- law firms,
- in-house counsel offices,
- government legal offices,
- nonprofits that employ lawyers,
- associations that serve the legal profession,
- law professors, and
- judges and court personnel.

It is for all of these key parts of our legal profession that this book has been written.

Student's Preface

Leadership for Lawyers can help students become better lawyers, possibly more than any single law school course or law
professor. As a first-year law student who had the privilege of
working on the first edition of this book, I found three things
very useful about the second edition. First, this book candidly
discusses some of the real challenges facing all of us in the legal
community. Second, it addresses these issues in a constructive
manner, showing how improving the leadership capabilities of
legal professionals could make a big difference in our
profession's capacity to deal with the challenges we face. Third,
the second edition recognizes that all legal organizations are also
businesses, influenced by ethics, tradition, and money. Recognizing that these factors affect daily practice makes *Leadership
for Lawyers* a very practical book. It forced me as a reader to
consider what values I wish to incorporate into my own legal
career and the barriers the legal profession as a whole may place
in my way.

 Leadership for Lawyers helped me think about the legal profession beyond my first-semester exams. It made me consider
the type of lawyer that I want to become and challenged me to
develop my leadership abilities. Law school encourages students
to take on leadership roles and to lead others in a responsible
and successful manner. The years we invest in learning the technical aspects of being a lawyer prepare us to assume leadership
roles in successful organizations in addition to making us proficient lawyers. All law students hope that our contributions in the
future as lawyers will help our clients, and our causes, achieve
even greater success. Being a better leader, I believe, will enable
us to provide even better legal services to those we serve. That
is why the section on leadership and organizational assessment
is so powerful for law students. The questions raised in this chap-

ter, used as part of a broader organizational assessment for legal organizations, will be the key questions that I ask potential employers.

Leadership for Lawyers helped me appreciate the importance of teamwork and mentoring in the legal community. From reading this book, I realized that I wanted to work in an office that values camaraderie and constructive feedback. Importantly, *Leadership for Lawyers* did not draw these conclusions for me, but rather laid out the legal profession in an organized and thorough manner, which allowed me to make these important conclusions for myself. *Leadership for Lawyers,* as much as any course I have taken, has provided me with critical tools and insights for a successful law school experience and legal career.

I think this book should be required reading for all law students and new members of the legal profession. It encouraged me to think critically about my future career and to use my time in law school to begin addressing areas of concern in modern legal practice. It has already improved my leadership skills, and I believe that *Leadership for Lawyers* can help create effective leaders by raising awareness of what it takes to be an effective leader. This is one book that can impact all levels of the legal profession. The need for effective leadership by lawyers permeates law firms, government offices, corporations, and nonprofit associates. All legal professionals can, and should, improve their leadership skills. This will make them better lawyers, will improve their communities, and will benefit the organizations that they may serve as board members or advisors. Although improving the leadership skills of everyone in our large profession is an ambitious goal for any one book, *Leadership for Lawyers* aims to accomplish this task one reader at a time.

Finally, I believe this book points the legal profession in the right direction in one other respect. We need to improve the public's perception of our profession's values and, specifically, its integrity. We require all law students to take an ethics course, and in many states lawyers must take continuing legal education classes year in and year out. We now require courses in professionalism before one can take a bar exam in some states and before one can be sworn in as a lawyer in others. Ethics and professionalism are two legs of a three-legged stool. Herb Rubenstein shows how leadership development is the third leg of this stool, which will make a huge difference in promoting higher standards of integrity and competence for lawyers. When lawyers become trained and skilled as better leaders, as I have by studying this book, we will have better integrity ourselves and will be better equipped to instill in the general populace the trust in our profession's integrity that the legal profession needs in order to remain a strong, positive influence on society. Hopefully, many others will find this book as useful and empowering as I have.

George Gilbert
Georgetown University Law Center

Acknowledgments

The reactions I have received over the years when I tell people I am writing a book on leadership for lawyers has run the entire gamut from full support to total disbelief. Both the first edition and this expanded second edition have gone far to quell the disbelievers. One category of disbelievers says that giving lawyers insights on leadership or leadership development training will not make them better lawyers. Another group thinks that lawyers are not really leaders anyway, since most of their time is spent advising clients and drafting agreements as instructed by decision makers. A third group thinks that lawyers are not interested in learning about leadership theory or improving their leadership capabilities.

There are many who have contributed to this book since 2001, when I embarked on an effort to bring to the legal profession the best of the leadership development literature and training. Bar associations in numerous states are starting to offer leadership development training, and some are even giving CLE credit for these educational and skill development programs. Successful lawyers like Ben Heineman, Jr., former GE vice-president for law and public affairs, now senior counsel at Wilmer Cutler Pickering Hale & Dorr, have recently started giving speeches on lawyers as leaders. Clearly, the legal profession is moving in the direction of other professions over the past decade, of realizing the importance that leadership development training can have in helping professionals perform their work more competently and have greater work satisfaction.

While my law professors and administrative staff from my alma mater, the Georgetown University Law Center, are far too numerous to mention, one person at Georgetown deserves to be singled out. Larry Center, the director of Georgetown's CLE program, who wrote the preface to the first and second editions of this book, deserves praise for standing in the forefront of promoting leadership development in the legal profession.

George Gilbert, a law student, who worked on the first edition and has written the "Student's Preface" to this edition, is to be thanked for his tireless work in compiling the Appendix comprised of approximately 90 brands of leadership, all explained cogently and usefully. George represents that new breed of law students who recognizes the value of learning to be a better leader.

Bruce Kirschner, of the Office of Personnel Management's Western Management Development Center, has been steadfast in his efforts to bring leadership development courses to lawyers in the federal government. Tom Grella, chair of the Law Practice Management Section (LPM) of the ABA, shows by example and support the true value of being a great leader in the legal profession. He and the LPM Section are dedicated to expanding leadership development training for all those in the legal profession.

Laura Rothacker wrote the chapter on "Women, Leadership, and the Legal Profession" for the first edition. Her keen insights are embedded in this edition's chapter on women. She has, through her deeds and her words, contributed greatly to this book and the legal profession.

Sam Cassidy is the primary author of the section on natural law in our chapter on ethics. He argues persuasively that lawyers must be knowledgeable regarding the basic tenets of natural law in order to give "principled advice to clients."

Jim Thompson, Amanda Foster, Steve Bloom, and Somerville Partners are to be thanked for their pathbreaking work on developing a leadership assessment instrument specifically for lawyers. Jim is the primary author of the chapter on leadership assessment.

There are many judges who may remember me as a litigator and who have guided my thinking, usually by interrupting me in the courtroom, and to them I would like to say a collective "thank you" and to acknowledge their dedicated leadership in the judiciary.

No book can be written for the American Bar Association without a champion at the ABA. Tim Brandhorst was enthusiastic about this project from the first day we discussed a possible role for the ABA in expanding the knowledge base of leadership development for lawyers. The ABA, with its Women in Law Leadership project and leadership development training, is bringing this concept of leadership development and its utility to the mainstream of the legal profession. To Tim and the ABA, all of your support is greatly appreciated.

There would be no book on leadership for lawyers if there were not lawyers who wanted to be better leaders. It is to you and your growing number that I owe the most gratitude. As you become a better leader, you will make the profession better and serve your clients more professionally. It is ultimately to you that I dedicate this book.

Leadership
FOR
LAWYERS

Second Edition

CHAPTER 1

The Case for Leadership Development for Lawyers

"Without leadership, nothing happens."

Fred Lederer, Chancellor Professor of Law, William and Mary Law School and Director of the Center for Legal and Court Technology, May 2007

Lawyers are called upon to lead every day. Although the lawyer is the "agent" and the client is the "principal," lawyers have a duty to lead their clients. They provide this leadership by providing accurate technical advice, principled counseling, and a rigorous evaluation of the client's situation, goals, and resources. This book is designed specifically for lawyers and all persons employed in the legal profession.

This book answers an important question raised by U.S. Judge James Barr. The question is:

> I am delving into whether there is support for the hypothesis that leadership skills developed and implemented by individual lawyers (even when not serving in bar organizations) can significantly impact and influence an entire legal community in such areas as (1) improved ethical and civility standards and performance, (2) more effective assimilation of new lawyers into the legal community, and (3) improved relations between bench and bar. In other words, I am at least curious about whether development of leadership skills by individual lawyers can positively impact the quality of lawyering in a legal community—even when working outside the institutional (i.e., bar organization) context.

This book answers Judge Barr's question in the affirmative. The basic thesis of this book is that when lawyers and all those who work in the legal profession begin to understand the basic theories of leadership and are better trained in the field of leadership development, they will become better leaders, will provide better legal services, and will create better law firms and legal organizations. As a consequence, the reputation of lawyers and the legal profession as a whole will improve.

This book is based on my work as a trial attorney for more than 20 years, handling matters for plaintiffs as well as defendants. I have practiced in three jurisdictions and argued and settled cases in literally hundreds of courtrooms. Most important, I have been hired by many clients not just to be a good technical lawyer, but to resolve difficult challenges through the use of well-developed leadership skills.

Leadership development training and education has evolved to the point where almost all professions can benefit from this new discipline. Are lawyers leaders? The answer is clearly "Yes." The general public, clients, and even other lawyers expect lawyers to be leaders not just because they know the law, but because so much faith is placed in their abilities to settle disputes, resolve complex legal challenges, establish new rules and regulations for society, and understand the complex and rugged landscape of litigation. However, because they are not well trained in leadership, many lawyers merely try to dominate the conversation in a manner that is neither productive nor satisfying for all concerned.

Lawyers are called upon to serve as members of boards of directors, boards of advisors, and boards of trustees; conduct high-level investigations into wrongdoing; uncover corruption; make high-stakes presentations to opposing counsel, government agencies, trial courts, and arbitration panels; and interact intelligently and cogently with the media. They are called upon to do research and negotiate regarding matters that can make or break the financial, emotional, and institutional lives and reputations of clients both large and small. The level of leadership required in each of these activities is extraordinary, yet the legal profession over the past 10 years has given continuing legal education credit to "creating Power Point presentations," but not leadership courses.

This book is designed to help those in the legal profession become better leaders. It is structured to help a lawyer objectively evaluate how good a leader he or she is today and creates a path to assist the lawyer in becoming a better leader in the future. The basic tenets of leadership that lawyers will learn can be applied both in client-oriented settings and in law firms and other organizational contexts where lawyers have responsibilities for leading and managing enterprises. This book is equally applicable for the solo practitioner, the in-house counsel, the plaintiff's bar, the defense bar (both civil and criminal), litigators, judges, arbitrators, real estate attorneys, environmental attorneys, bankruptcy attorneys, intellectual property attorneys, lawyers who work for government agencies, lawyers who conduct investigations, securities attorneys, and merger and acquisition attorneys, as well as bond counsel, international trade attorneys, food and drug attorneys, and tax attorneys. It was written for partners, associates, chairmen and chairwomen of large and small law firms, solo practitioners, judges, law students, and law professors. It may be unrealistic to think that law schools will ever start offering many classes on leadership, given the amount of information law schools have to teach students in three years (or four years for night students) to give them a fighting chance to pass the bar exam.

Harvard University Law School has a course offered by Philip Heymann called Leadership in the Public Sector. Professor Heymann is on record as recommending that every law school teach at least one course in leadership. Another law school, at the University of Santa Clara, offers a leadership course for law students. We hope that this book could be a worthy text for such courses. At present, the teaching of leadership knowledge and skills is left up to those lawyers who take courses outside the legal profession and are self-taught. This book and the courses based on this text to be taught by the U.S. Office of Personnel Management and other schools represent an opening for lawyers into a new world of leadership theories and practical suggestions regarding how to be a better leader, and thereby a better lawyer.

There are significant developments in the teaching of leadership for lawyers. The Cincinnati Bar Association has had a Leadership for Lawyers course for some time. The Alabama Supreme Court has instituted a leadership program for lawyers. The Business Law Institute of the Colorado Bar Association has created a leadership seminar. The American Psychological Association in 2004 published a book, *Lawyer Know Thyself*, which discusses personality strengths and weaknesses with a view toward assisting lawyers to be better leaders. Courses in professionalism and ethics touch on leadership behaviors and values. Bar associations and the ABA have leadership classes designed to help lawyers become better leaders within those organizations. The Oregon Bar Association has a leadership development program for new lawyers. The Renaissance Lawyer Society promotes stronger leadership development among lawyers to help address some of the ills that currently affect the legal profession. And now blogs are starting to address leadership development for lawyers. Although some "leadership" articles and courses are merely marketing and business development courses in disguise, we are finding that leadership development courses increasingly are getting to the core of what makes a lawyer a better leader.

Problems and Challenges of the Legal Profession

The problems and challenges that currently beset the legal profession are well known within the industry but not deeply understood by most lawyers, their clients, or the law schools whose curriculum has become more technical in nature during the past 20 years. These problems include:

- High rates of dissatisfaction among young attorneys
- Poor reputation of lawyers within society
- High departure rate for lawyers from the legal profession
- Growing economic pressures on law firms of all sizes, especially large ones
- High levels of client dissatisfaction and formal complaints and malpractice actions against lawyers
- Growing levels of associate turnover
- "Burnout," causing lawyers to leave the profession entirely
- Prevalence of outdated governance practices at law firms
- Continuing evidence of a glass ceiling for women in law firms
- Client challenges to increasingly large legal bills and insistence on alternative billing structures
- Growing numbers of ethical complaints against lawyers
- Increasing competition and growing use of questionable means to obtain clients/business
- Increasing lack of civility among lawyers
- Increasing delays in litigation, arbitrations, and even mediations

7

- Lack of training in leadership in a profession whose members lead clients and organizations, serve on boards of directors, and hold high political and governmental positions, all without the benefit of the knowledge created in the field of leadership during the past 25 years
- High levels of substance abuse among lawyers, affecting their ability to serve clients' needs

These challenges dominate discussions at bar association conferences. Leadership development training on the practical aspects of how lawyers and all persons who work in the legal profession can improve their leadership skills will help address some, if not all, of these challenges currently so significant in the legal profession.

The legal industry is one of the most rapidly growing professions in the world. From 1950 to 2005, the legal profession grew faster than almost any other industry in the United States. Record numbers of law graduates, record numbers of practicing attorneys, record numbers of women entering the profession, record salaries for private practitioners, record numbers of large jury awards, and increasingly large average jury verdicts propelled a growing profession to stay busy and self-confident, and not to reflect on the growing challenges in a maturing industry. Today, the legal profession is challenged by competitive pressures from technology that puts the law, statutes, court decisions, and legal procedures at the fingertips of anyone who has access to the Internet. Clients can perform more of their own work and are much better informed than ever before. In-house legal counsel, with capital to spend on computers and databases, have taken back significant amounts of work from major law firms. Lawyers can advertise and attract clients based on the quality of their advertising rather than on the quality of their abilities as a lawyer. The insurance industry has succeeded in securing new legislative caps on medical malpractice awards, on pain and suffering awards of all kinds, and judges are beginning to impose "loser pay" rules in domestic relations and other types of cases. Mergers of law firms, unheard of just 20 years ago, are moving forward at a fever pitch, resulting in law firms with over 1,000 employees. These financial and industry statistics all point to societal and economic pressures that will soon challenge every aspect of the legal profession economically and organizationally.

Leadership Development for Many Groups in the Legal Profession

Today, leadership development is essential not only to those who try to lead these mega-firms, but also to solo practitioners and lawyers in small firms who rely on their leadership contributions in their communities as a significant element of their business development and reputation-enhancing activities. And, as in-house counsel are more often expected to sit at the strategy table, leadership development for this subsection of the legal profession has become a critical component of the skill set they need to perform their jobs and be leaders in their organizations.

The Sarbanes-Oxley legislation has placed those lawyers who counsel corporations on governance, audit, and financial disclosure/reporting issues in the position of being "leaders of leaders," a term that will be extensively discussed in this book. As the Sarbanes-Oxley principles are extended to the nonprofit world, academic institutions, and eventually to governments at all levels, lawyers' leadership skills will be severely tested, as they will be expected to be not only the messenger of change, but also the guide leading organizations into the brave new world of significant governance oversight.

The legal profession is already struggling mightily with new and subtle changes to the attorney-client privilege caused by lawyers knowing about fraudulent financial activities of their clients. The new role of independent directors who demand that the company's lawyers tell them what previously would have been attorney-client privileged and never told to "outsiders" is making lawyers gain a deeper understanding of what it means to be a leader in a disclosure-rich world.

9

All of these developments in the legal profession argue mightily that lawyers should seek, and the legal profession should offer, the best leadership development education and training possible. This book is a start. Many lawyers will use it to begin or expand their quest to become better leaders. And law firms, professional legal organizations, law students, and those who are considering law school will use it to achieve a competitive advantage over other law firms, law students, and fellow lawyers who do not seek to improve their leadership skills.

Finally, after reading this book, one might consider taking either an individual leadership assessment questionnaire or an organizational leadership assessment survey. These will be discussed in our chapter on leadership assessment. Many leadership assessment tools have existed for years, and now such tools are being developed specifically for lawyers and those who work in the legal profession.

This book will serve as a guide to learning about the leadership development literature, successful leadership behaviors, and how lawyers and those who work in the legal profession can use their newly enhanced leadership skills to improve themselves and the profession. By reading this book, practitioners should expect to improve both their lawyering skills and their ability to lead and manage clients and organizations.

Conclusion

A review of the major theories of leadership and of those leadership behaviors that have withstood the test of time is a solid place from which to begin. Two stories from our profession help to guide us through the reasons why leadership is so important for lawyers and those in the legal profession.

There was a time not many years ago when a person in California could not hold both a license to practice law and a license to be a certified public accountant. A lawyer named Jay Foonberg successfully challenged this law. In America, he could not see how and why such a law could stand. Through his work, the prohibition of holding both professional licenses—in law and as a CPA—was dismantled. Similarly, in the early 1980s, on the books of the Virginia Supreme Court, there was a rule that no one would be allowed to take the Virginia Bar or waive into the Virginia Bar unless he or she lived in Virginia or promised to earn 100% of his or her income from a Virginia office. A legal challenge by a female law student proved successful in removing this unjust rule. I was among the first beneficiaries of her leadership when I became a member of the Virginia Bar in 1983 while living in Washington, D.C. History is full of rights that have been won by lawyers who are leaders. Women are now starting to make real progress in obtaining the leadership positions they have deserved in our profession for decades.

Law firms from the past have stories of their founding partners winning that precedent-setting case or obtaining that marquee client through which the firm was able to grow to greatness. Today, leadership is different. As we move from old leadership theories that posited greatness on one person, we now focus on theories that emphasize how groups of people are able to work together to produce greatness. Information technology enables everyone to become a participant in key decisions that affect legal organizations, but only if the current leaders allow this important use of technology. The basic underpinnings of the new emphasis on inclusive leadership in the legal profession could not have been possible without electronic communication and storage of information; without our ability to communicate, reason, and negotiate across large distances in nanoseconds; and without the fast pace of technological improvements.

Underpinning all aspects of leadership are values and ethics. Our Ethics section includes a lengthy discussion of the basic tenets of natural law, which are as relevant to lawyers and the entire legal profession as they were when written hundreds of years ago. Finally, upon reading this book, you are invited to make a commitment to become a student of leadership as well as a practitioner by taking leadership development courses, whether they are for CLE credit or not. As Edward Poll stated in his recent article, "Making Law Firm Leadership More Effective," in *Law Practice Today* (April 2007), the magazine of ABA's Law Practice Management Section, "The most important function of all law firm leadership is to facilitate continuous communication. . . . Today, the larger law firm . . . must have clearly defined roles of leadership."

Chapter Two will provide the reader with a strong grounding in leadership theory, in understanding basic areas of leadership competence, and in becoming familiar with how to be successful in the key area of motivation. Lawyers are leaders, and training is required in every profession to enhance critical skills. Leadership is now a critical skill of lawyers and those who work in the legal profession.

CHAPTER 2

Leadership Theory and Practice for the Legal Profession

"Clients and prospective clients want to do business with leaders, and anything you can do to further develop and enhance your leadership skills and your leadership profile will benefit you in your business development efforts."

Jeffrey L. Nischwitz, *Think Again! Innovative Approaches to the Business of Law,* ABA, Law Practice Management Section (Chicago, 2007)

What is leadership? *Leadership is the creation and fulfillment of worthwhile opportunities by honorable means.*

There are more than 300 published definitions of leadership. There are thousands of books on leadership, 10 generally accepted theories of leadership, and several theories regarding motivation, an important subset of leadership. This chapter is a concise review of the leadership literature for lawyers, law students, and those who work in the legal profession.

One basic notion of leadership particularly applicable to the legal profession is *problem solving*. Leaders are people who solve problems, and often see problems and understand them before others recognize they are problems. One important skill set for a lawyer is to analyze a client's course of action and be able to predict, and find ways around, expected legal problems and challenges that may thwart a client from achieving his or her goals.

There are approximately 90 "brands" of leadership described in Appendix A of this book. There are 10 specific theories of leadership, but no general theory. Each of these leadership theories tries to explain how leaders become leaders, or how leaders work when they are leading people. The first nine theories are based on Northouse's work on leadership and are presented in evolutionary order: each theory builds on the previous theory. The tenth theory is a contribution to the leadership literature by this author, and dates back to Jethro in the *Book of Exodus*. The 10 leadership theories are as follows:

Leadership Theory

1. The Trait Theory: People with certain favorable physical, mental, personality, and emotional traits are more likely, if not destined, to be leaders.
2. The Style Approach: Leadership is a function of the style of behavior a person brings to a situation. Typical styles of leadership activity include Team Management, Authority Compliance, Country Club Management, and Impoverished Management.
3. The Situational Approach: Leaders must "read" a situation accurately and determine what combination of supportive and directive behaviors is appropriate to achieve the goal of the leader. This theory suggests that leaders adapt their styles and behavior based on understanding the full content and context of the situation in which they

are operating, their role, the goals of the situation, and the resources they have to use and direct.

4. The Contingency Theory: Understanding and developing successful leadership behaviors is based on analyzing three key factors: leader-member relations, task structure, and position power. Contingency theory shows how the success of certain styles of leadership is contingent on the circumstances in which they are used. Thus, this theory suggests that the relationship between the leaders and the followers should have a strong impact on the leader and the appropriate leadership style that will be effective in that situation.

5. Path-Goal Theory: This is the motivational theory of leadership. This theory suggests that a major goal of leadership is to stimulate performance and satisfaction among those led by the leader. Under this theory, the classic behaviors of the leader are (1) to identify goals and to secure "buy-in," support, enthusiasm, and ownership of these goals by the followers; (2) to identify all key obstacles and barriers to achieving goals; (3) to ensure proper training and resources for followers in their effort to achieve goals; (4) to organize and direct the actions of the followers in their efforts to achieve goals; (5) to monitor all activity and guide any changes in strategy, resources, and actions necessary to achieve goals; (6) to identify precisely and accurately when the goal is achieved or the shortcomings that result from the effort; (7) to acknowledge and systematically reward all followers for contributions in the effort to achieve goals; and (8) to set new goals and expectations for the group and repeat the process.

6. Leader-Member Exchange Theory: Leadership is a function of a relationship in which followers give to a leader leadership status and responsibilities and the leader accepts that status and performs leadership acts that the followers accept. The relationship between the leader and followers is one of partnership rather than control. Power

15

is equally shared by members with the leader, and the leader's ability and authority to lead is always a function of the support he or she has from the members.

7. Transformational Leadership: Leadership is a process where leaders and followers work together in a manner that changes and transforms individuals and groups. It is a dynamic process that assesses the followers' needs and motives and seeks the input of the followers at each critical stage in the leadership process. Transformational leadership presupposes that the goal of the leader is to promote change and improvement for the betterment and with the assistance of the followers. This type of leadership has an explicit goal of turning followers into future leaders.

8. Team Leadership: This theory assumes that all leaders are leaders of teams and the major functions of a leader are (1) to help the group determine which goals and tasks it wants to achieve; (2) to help create enabling processes and direct the group so that it achieves the goals and tasks; (3) to keep the group (and the leader) supplied with the right resources, training, and supplies; (4) to set standards for behavior, success, and ethics; (5) to diagnose and remedy group deficiencies; (6) to forecast impending environmental changes to help inform and steer the group appropriately; and (7) to help maintain and defend the group by organizing it and ensuring its proper internal functioning.

9. Psychodynamic Approach: Leadership requires that leaders understand their own psychological makeup and the psychological makeup of those they lead. Leaders using this theory are those who understand (1) the followers' attitudes, potential, behaviors, and expected responses to leadership; (2) the level of maturity of followers and its impact on their responses to leadership actions; (3) the desires and motivational keys of followers; (4) the meaning and interpretation by followers of language, behavior, symbols, and situations; (5) the proper balance of de-

pendence and independence appropriate for a given group of followers; (6) the proper psychological relationship between the leader and followers; and (7) of the psychodynamic interplay between the leader and followers and between and among leaders as well.

10. Leaders of Leaders: This theoretical construct states that the job of a leader of followers is completely different from that of a leader of leaders. Leaders of followers are mainly problem solvers. Leaders of leaders establish platforms and seek to create an environment so that followers can act as leaders themselves, solve their own problems, and make excellent decisions consistent with the platform that the leader of leaders sets. In addition, the leaders of leaders concept incorporates the idea that the platform set by the leader of leaders will improve over time because the followers and other leaders will be encouraged to test the platform in the real world, find deficiencies, and report proposed improvements for the platform to the leader of leaders. The major role of the leader of leaders is to create this platform and not to make decisions in particular situations. This job is delegated to the leaders whom the leader of leaders leads.

Leadership Actions

Are lawyers leaders? The answer is clearly yes. To be a better leader, one needs to become familiar with examples of leadership behaviors that have proven successful over time. Within each category and specific behavioral item listed in this chapter, there is much room for individual variations and creativity. However, there is little room for the leader of a law firm, a leader of legal organizations, a leader of clients, or an advocate for a client to ignore the items listed below and still achieve passing marks in leadership. There are approximately 60 behaviors that researchers believe constitute good leadership practices.

A great example of leadership in the legal profession occurred over the past several years in the area of tax law. A major law firm was approached by a very large accounting firm and asked to draft legal opinions of various tax shelters proposed by the accounting firm. The law firm was eminently qualified to do the work. The potential fees were huge. The matter was very attractive to the law firm.

After careful deliberation, the firm's management decided not to undertake the work. Numerous lawyers within the firm were not happy with the decision, but the way the law firm went about making the decision and the basis for its position showed that it was a true leader in the field of tax law in the United States. The reason the law firm chose not to accept the work was that the tax shelter structures and operations, in the firm's opinion, violated several important principles of tax law in the United States. Ultimately, it came to a conclusion: *No law firm in the United States should undertake this work.*

Only a law firm that believes it is a leader in the field of tax law could ever reach the conclusion that no law firm in the United States should undertake this lucrative work from a reputable accounting firm. But being a leader in the field of tax law made it perfectly clear that this major law firm could not undertake the work regardless of the size of the fees and the reputation of the potential client.

Another firm did take on this work. That accounting firm and a lawyer working on these matters have been indicted. The law firm that turned down the work now enjoys the benefits of a clear decision generated, in significant part, because it knew and acted as a leader in the field of tax law, rather than as a law firm that would do whatever a client asked it to do. Here, true leadership, with its huge short-term costs in lost revenue, paid enormous dividends.

Benjamin Heineman, Jr., in his November 2006 lecture, "Lawyers as Leaders," at Yale Law School, made it clear that lawyers must find congruence between their values and the work they perform. Citing statistics that showed that lawyers were 3.5 times more depressed than the average of the other 105 professions studied, Heineman suggested that lawyers were able, and well trained intellectually, to become leaders and take positions in society where they made decisions, in addition to merely advising decision makers. In every lawyer's career, advising others is critical, but so is making significant decisions and managing the process where those decisions are carried out. In his lecture, Heineman stated:

> We are seeking lawyers who are not just strong team members but who can lead and build organizations: create the vision, the values, the priorities, the strategies, the people, the systems, the processes, the checks and balances, the resources and the motivation. Working on teams and leading them are interconnected: much of leadership today is not command and control of the troops but persuasion and motivation and empowerment of teams around a shared vision. . . .
>
> The concept of being a lawyer should encompass the broadest kind of leadership because our core skills, properly conceived, of understanding how values, rules and institutions interrelate with social, economic and political conditions is as central to the demands of leadership as any other professional or disciplinary background.

The call is clear. The opportunity for a lawyer to be a leader is present every day. The duty is also obvious. Clients look to us to be leaders. Although more than half of all lawyers are solo practitioners, they serve on boards for their clients and in community organizations, and all lawyers, including solo practitioners, have leadership challenges. Checklists are simply guideposts to help people identify areas they need to consider in their efforts to lead. The checklists below can help lawyers and those in the legal profession realize they have blind spots regarding how to lead. You can use these checklists to rate yourself on a scale of 1 to 10, with 1 being very poor and 10 being outstanding. More detailed work on leadership evaluation appears in Chapter Six of this book.

In a speech to the Law Practice Management Section of the ABA in 2007, Thomas A. Edmonds, who served for 18 years as the executive director and chief operating officer of the Virginia

Bar Association, provided the following list of key attributes and activities of leaders in the legal profession whom he had observed over his long career. As a member of the Virginia bar during his full term, I can attest that many of these attributes and activities apply directly to Mr. Edmonds and his very successful tenure at the helm of the Virginia State Bar.

A leader in the legal profession is one who:

- Is a visionary
- Gets buy-in
- Gives direction
- Is not dictatorial
- Is collaborative
- Has courage
- Exercises sound judgment
- Is discreet
- Has an impact
- Keeps commitments
- Has humility
- Acknowledges others
- Has an innovative spirit
- Is adaptable
- Has tenacity
- Has integrity
- Focuses on the future

From the leadership literature we see these attributes and activities of leaders, plus many more, organized into five categories in the checklists below.

Checklist 1: People Management

A successful leader is one who:

❏ Clearly communicates expectations

❏ Recognizes, acknowledges, and rewards achievement

❏ Inspires others and serves as a catalyst for others to perform in ways they would not undertake without the leader's support and direction

❏ Puts the right people in the right positions at the right time with the right resources and the right job descriptions

❏ Secures alignment on what is the right direction for the organization

❏ Persuades and encourages people in the organization to achieve the desired results for the organization

❏ Makes sure not to "burn out" people in the organization, looking out for their well-being as well as the well-being of the organization

❏ Identifies weak signals that suggest impending conflict within the organization and attacks the sources of conflict effectively

❏ Holds people accountable

❏ Encourages the human capital development of every person in the organization through training, mentoring, and education, and allocates sufficient resources to this endeavor

❏ Correctly evaluates the actual performance and the potential of each person in the organization

❏ Encourages people in the organization to stand up for and express their beliefs

❏ Creates a non-fear-based environment in which all persons in the organization can speak the truth as they see it without concern for retaliation

❏ Delegates

❏ Is able to have rapport and empathize with those he or she leads

Checklist 2: Strategic Management

A successful leader is one who:

❏ Is flexible when necessary to adapt to changing circumstances

❏ Sets, with input from others including all stakeholders, the long-term direction for the organization

❏ Understands the organization's competitive environment, social trends, competitors, customers, and all stakeholders

❏ Correctly analyzes the potential risks of all decisions

❏ Correctly analyzes the potential returns of all decisions

❏ Has the ability to focus on specific problems without losing his or her ability to see at the outer edges, gathering worthwhile information that others miss or fail to see as significant or relevant

❏ Understands the strengths and weaknesses of the organization and how to exploit the strengths and address the weaknesses successfully

❏ Develops and implements strategies to improve the strengths and to combat the weaknesses of the organization

❏ Identifies appropriate partners, strategic alliances, and outside resources to tap in order to help further the organization's goals

❏ Articulates the values of the organization and develops strategies consistent with these core values

❏ Demonstrates a strong commitment to diversity and positive change

❏ Demonstrates a strong commitment to creating and sustaining a learning organization (learning is the foundation for all sustainable change)

Checklist 3: Personal Characteristics

A successful leader is one who:

- ❏ Lives with honesty and integrity
- ❏ Selects people for his or her team who are honest and have high integrity
- ❏ Has the will, passion, and desire to succeed
- ❏ Possesses a willingness to shoulder the responsibility for success (without being a "thunder taker") and failure (without casting blame)
- ❏ Is innovative and open to new ideas
- ❏ Is not willing to accept the ways things are because they can always be improved; is never satisfied completely with the status quo
- ❏ Is smart, intelligent, emotionally strong
- ❏ Is confident without being arrogant
- ❏ Is an able negotiator
- ❏ Is willing to be patient
- ❏ Is decisive when necessary
- ❏ Is able to think analytically
- ❏ Learns quickly
- ❏ Is respectful to all
- ❏ Is perceptive and sensitive to the needs of others
- ❏ Demonstrates diligence, discipline, and strong perseverance capabilities
- ❏ Is comfortable with ambiguity
- ❏ Is willing to be original
- ❏ Takes informed and intelligent risks

Checklist 4: Process Management

A successful leader is one who:

- ❑ Manages change
- ❑ Promotes innovation
- ❑ Secures resources
- ❑ Allocates resources wisely
- ❑ Solves problems well
- ❑ Anticipates crises
- ❑ Handles crises well when they explode
- ❑ Creates and manages budgets well
- ❑ Creates and manages timelines and work plans
- ❑ Possesses and manifests great project management skills
- ❑ Translates long-term visions into step-by-step plans
- ❑ Measures results and reports them accurately
- ❑ Recognizes quickly when a process or activity is not working
- ❑ Redesigns processes as often as necessary to be successful

---

These leadership behaviors and categories apply to lawyers and people in the legal profession just as they apply to leaders in every profession and organization. Knowing the full extent of this checklist may remind the lawyer and those in the legal profession of the importance of certain leadership behaviors that they may not have considered important in the past. Each skill or ability can be learned and improved. Self-awareness of one's strengths and weaknesses is a first step toward improvement and improving leadership. This list of leadership behaviors can be used by all types of legal organizations as criteria to evaluate their employees and their leaders. Workshops and seminars can be taken to improve each of these skills and we recommend that such education and training programs be approved for CLE credit. Now we turn to an area of leadership that has not received much attention in the legal profession: *motivation*.

Motivation Explained and Demonstrated

Lawyers working with clients and colleagues are often called upon to help motivate colleagues, clients, subordinates, and those who supervise their work. Leaders who are successful in motivating others:

- Recognize and avoid burnout in oneself and others
- Improve the ability of participants to delegate and achieve results through the work and cooperation of others
- Articulate and understand group dynamics, followership, and factors in communications styles, strategies, and content that affect the response of others
- Recognize the power of building long-lasting professional relationships
- Implement strategies to create and elicit rapport
- Appreciate the value of one's reputation and its relationship to motivation
- Call forth the leadership potential in others and in oneself
- Know the role of fair and equitable treatment of others in achieving and maintaining high motivation

Motivation is a critical component of leadership. In the legal community, lawyers and leaders of legal organizations are called upon every day to motivate associates, staff, court clerks, and personnel to perform their duties well, motivate their clients to help gather facts and witnesses, and motivate themselves to serve as models in the community. Although people may believe that teaching motivation skills is difficult, this chapter has outlined many of the basic elements that go into successful efforts to motivate others. Lawyers and people working in the legal profession with their heavy work schedules, demanding clients and judges, challenging cases, and large areas of responsibility would be well served to become better motivators. Each person in the legal profession will need to find an approach to motivation that works in a repeatable fashion over time. Motivation is a key element in avoiding burnout and in producing great results in teams and workplaces. Lawyers are faced with one type of a motivation-oriented problem that is rarely faced by other professionals. Because lawyers work in an adversary system, lawyers must often motivate their adversaries, motivate third parties such as juries and judges, and motivate government agencies and other tribunals to treat their clients fairly. Thus, the arenas where lawyers earn their living have special motivation-oriented challenges far beyond the challenges faced by most workers and most professions in our economy.

Conclusion

We like to think that legal matters are technical in nature. They are, in part. But the lawyers are actors in the role of leaders, and the judges and arbitrators are in the ultimate leadership role, deciding who is telling the truth and who is not. Today, it is fair to say that whenever any judge states that he or she finds that a witness is not credible, the party who called that witness loses. Integrity is not the hallmark of a leader just because it is a lofty goal of the few who can reach the high status of a leader. Rather, integrity is the hallmark of a leader because leaders know that integrity works, day in and day out.

Lawyers are leaders because they are willing to take on huge responsibilities for important legal matters. Leaders are people who are willing to take responsibility for an outcome. Leaders pull together teams to accomplish results. Lawyers do this every day. The checklists in this chapter are merely that—lists of areas of concern and activities of leaders. We do many of these without thinking, but we fail to do others because we do not think about them on a regular basis. Leaders do not cut corners on these checklists. As you evaluate yourself or others on leadership, these checklists are a good starting ground for you to review the leadership behaviors of yourself and others. There are certainly more items that should be on the checklist. Add to this list those activities that you believe leaders who are lawyers should undertake on a regular basis.

These activities are different from leadership competencies, which will be discussed in a later chapter. Competencies are the skills that help leaders lead. Activities are what leaders do. Lawyers face enormous time pressures in their work, and some bill in six-minute increments. One could reasonably ask, "How can I perform all of these leadership activities given the limited time that I can devote to any particular task?" That is a fair question, and there are two good answers. Many of the activities of leadership take very little time. In fact, many are timesavers because if they are not done, mistakes or problems occur that take far longer to fix than leading properly in the first place. Second, the idea that you are the only leader is an idea whose time has long gone. Leaders train and help others to learn these activities so that they can lead and undertake more responsibilities. The last activity in the area of people management is "delegate." Leaders must know to whom to delegate and when to delegate and how to monitor but not micromanage those to whom they delegate duties, responsibility, and even authority. Once trained in leadership, those to whom you delegate duties can often successfully perform the role of leader regarding those activities.

Explaining the theories of leadership could easily be a book in itself. Our overview here has one goal. Lawyers can begin to master the basic theories of leadership in very short order. Knowing these theories allows those in the legal profession to have a solid footing in the field of leadership development. It allows them to begin to teach leadership to others and to recognize and learn from great leadership when they see it. Leadership is a lifelong endeavor that requires lifelong learning. Not all actions by leaders, even with integrity, good intentions, meticulously drafted plans, and adequate resources, will be successful. But all leadership actions, when informed by the checklists and theories discussed above, will have a better chance of succeeding than leadership actions that fail to take into account the complex and dynamic aspects of leadership embodied here.

CHAPTER 3

Women, Leadership, and the Legal Profession

"Most lawyers know how to negotiate for their clients. This course will teach you how to negotiate for yourself."

A Leadership Development Program for Women Law Partners (2007), Brochure for the The Hastings Leadership Academy for Women

Recent developments in the past two years show clearly that women are making substantial progress in achieving leadership positions in the legal profession. There are now seminars on leadership development specifically for women in the legal profession. The creation of the Women in Law Leadership Academy by the ABA Commission on Women in the Profession, the election of the third woman president of the ABA, and the number of recent books on how women can break down the barriers they face in the legal profession is growing. In addition, in 2007 the Women's Law Association of Harvard University held its inaugural conference, "Rewriting the Rules: The Paradox of

Success as an HLS Woman." The conference invited women law graduates from Harvard to address the past successes and current large-scale challenges that women are facing in the legal profession. We predict over the next five years an explosion of conferences, seminars, books, articles, blog content, and increased law school and law firm attention to the fate of women in law. What is being done in the summer of 2007 at the University of California at Hastings, quoted above, will be done hundreds of times all over the country in the coming years. The intersection of the growing force of women in the legal profession and the growing need for leadership development training for all those in the legal profession, including women, is creating a huge demand for such leadership development courses for women. This book, and especially this chapter, are no substitute for intensive leadership development training for women to advance their careers, their effectiveness, and their impact on the legal profession. This book and this chapter are introductions for many women to the real benefits that will accrue to them by substantially improving their leadership development skills and talents.

One example of an article written in *The New York Times* in April 2007 epitomizes the evolution of women to greater leadership status in the legal profession. Titled "Female Lawyers Set Sights on Yet One More Goal: A Seat on the Board," the article cites that only 14% of *Fortune* 500 companies have women on their board as of 2006. The DirectWomen Institute, created in 2007 and sponsored in part by the American Bar Association, seeks to help promote women to board seats in these companies. As women seek to expand their leadership roles in the legal profession, many women who have already achieved leadership positions as partners in major law firms are seeking to leverage their success to become leaders of major companies in the United States.

With women graduating at well over 50% of the total law student classes for the past 15 years and fewer than 20% of all partners in law firms being women, there is consensus that women are simply not adequately represented in leadership roles in the legal profession. The role of women in the legal profession is at a crossroads. The existence of a huge disconnect between the large number of women in the profession and the small number of women who occupy positions of authority is analogous to the huge role black athletes play in professional sports and the limited role they play in positions of authority. The experiences of one of the contributors to this chapter, an attorney who commenced her career as one of the first women attorneys serving as in-house counsel in a large insurance company and who later became a senior partner in one of the largest law firms in Denver, was essential to gathering the information necessary to write this chapter and putting all of this information into context. This is a chapter written about women, with substantial contributions by a woman who has been there and is dedicated to improving both the legal profession and the role of women in it.

In this chapter, we explore systemic issues that contribute to the shortage of women in leadership positions in both major and medium-size law firms in the United States. In addition to a review of the literature on women in the legal profession, we conducted a survey of women lawyers designed to elicit information regarding the current status of women in leadership positions and the differences in leadership styles between male and female attorneys.

The first woman admitted to a state bar (Iowa) in 1869 saw her quest to bcome a lawyer foiled by the United States Supreme Court in a decision in 1873 that declared women "unfit for the law." Arabella Mansfield was the first in a long line of women who were denied admission to practice law in various states. Women were regularly denied admission to law schools during the late 1800s and early 1900s. Until the 1960s and early 1970s, many law schools strictly limited the admission of women. This changed with the passage of Title IX in 1975, which was not fully implemented by many law schools for several years. In 1978, a raging debate at many law schools was whether law firms should be banned from conducting interviews if their stated policy was that male law students were to be interviewed for associate positions, while women law students were to be interviewed only for legal secretary positions. Such blatant sexual discrimination seems not only absurd in 1978, it was especially absurd for a profession that prides itself on being a leader in promoting fairness and equality in our society.

Until recently, women practicing law faced overt discrimination in this male-dominated profession. To understand the current issues facing women, it is important to acknowledge that much has changed for the better over the past 20 years. In spite of this progress, systemic issues remain prevalent in society, as well as in the legal profession, that act to preclude women from significant leadership positions.

Historically, the predominant style of leadership and advocacy in the male-dominated legal profession was one of control and subordination. The central characteristic of this leadership style was a top-down command style that controlled subordinates through aggressive dominance.

As the number of women in the legal profession grew during the 1970s and 1980s, women lawyers were expected by male senior partners to emulate men in all outward respects if they wanted to rise to leadership in the firm. Many women dressed like men, in dark suits with silk bow ties. Women began to use sports metaphors and patiently listened to sexually explicit and frequently offensive jokes by male counterparts. During this period, women believed that if they "proved themselves," this type of behavior would become a thing of the past.

In greater and greater numbers since 1970, women have proven themselves in the legal profession. As a result, much of the overt discrimination has disappeared. Unfortunately, it was not due to the mentoring and guidance of the male senior members of firm that made this possible. It was the dedication, loyalty, and praise for women lawyers from clients using the legal services of women attorneys that made men in the legal profession realize that women could be very successful lawyers as well as strong leaders in the profession.

The success of women and the support of their clients in both the legal and business worlds permitted women to achieve a measure of freedom from the authoritarian leadership style of the male-dominated profession. In many cases, when women became partners in firms, it was because they adapted male stereotypes of behavior and had strong, vocal support from their clients. As the evolution of women in the legal workplace began to take hold in the 1980s, many women began to liberate themselves from the need to act "like the men." This courageous act freed those women from the outward requirements of male-oriented appearance and style.

With the growing professional success of women throughout the 1970s, 1980s, and 1990s, and the enormous increase in the number of women attending law schools and graduating at or near the top of their classes, one would reasonably have expected a commensurate increase in the number of women taking over traditional leadership roles in the legal profession. This was not the case in the latter part of the last century, and it is still not the case today. Although there are many strong women in leadership positions in the legal profession, the numbers are not statistically representative of the aggregate number of women who are practicing law. In this chapter we explore some of the reasons why women are not reaching the top of the profession of law today.

Collaborative Leadership

The old style of leadership both in business and law, and as most recently exhibited by our fellow attorney, John Bolton, is the "kiss up and kick down" form of leadership. This style of leadership has proven to be shortsighted for those who want to lead in an empowering, ethical, and effective manner. In 2005, this style was flatly rejected by the U.S. Senate in refusing to confirm Bolton's nomination as ambassador to the United Nations.

Most academic treatises on leadership and scholars of leadership development agree that the collaborative style of leadership is much more effective in a world of diverse populations and rapidly changing paradigms. Collaborative or transformational leadership, as its title implies, is centered on discussion rather than one-way commands, persuasion rather than dictating, empowering rather than subordinating people, and partnering rather than controlling or threatening, to achieve a goal. Transformational leadership, as espoused by Burns and others, cites the key role of leaders as helping their followers become leaders themselves as a direct result of their participation in leadership activities. The role of the collaborative leader or transformational leader is to enhance and maximize the skills and contribution of each team member to create the best result. The collaborative leader is responsible for keeping the team operating efficiently and staying on task. The collaborative or transformational leader is responsible for making sure that all followers are given the resources they need to be effective. Collaborative leaders take primary responsibility for resolving and heading off all major conflicts within the group. Collaborative leaders actively create opportunities for subordinates and followers to grow, mature, and transform into leaders in their own right.

Both research and the experiential data document the fact that women excel as collaborative leaders. In comprehensive studies of senior men and women executives conducted by Robert Kabacoff, Ph.D., of the Management Research Group, senior women executives were rated by peers, bosses, and independently as:

- Having a greater degree of energy, intensity, and emotional expression
- Having a greater capacity to keep others enthusiastic and involved
- More likely to set deadlines and monitor progress to ensure the completion of activities
- Setting higher expectations for performance for both themselves and others

The implications of these findings cannot be exaggerated. When the leadership style of the legal profession shifts from command and control to collaborative, as we predict it will over the next several decades, women will be uniquely poised to take advantage of this change. And, as more women succeed in reaching leadership positions in the business world, one can be assured that many of these women business leaders will seek out and hire women attorneys who share their values and leadership styles.

Certainly, men can also be excellent collaborative leaders. These men regularly choose the best attorneys (men and women) for projects based upon their expertise and give them significant authority over their part of the transaction. They solicit and take the advice of others who work on their legal teams. They include the client as an integral part of the decision-making team. They practice inclusive leadership, getting the best from all who participate. Lawyers who practice collaborative leadership make sure that they do not take an autocratic role in the effort to serve the client and perform their duties as a lawyer and counselor. They excel at being facilitators, mediators, and consummate litigators, as well as deal makers. They create a loyal client base and associates whom they help grow into leadership capabilities and positions. Collaborative leaders are those in the legal profession who are helping to pave the way for women to become leaders in the legal profession. Our experience suggests that they are growing in number in the profession, though we could not find any research specifically on this aspect of leadership. Yet, it is not too great a generalization to state that experience has shown and still shows that men in the legal profession, be they associates or managing partners, are frequently steered or mentored toward the old-fashioned, masculine styles of leadership.

Based upon our own experiences and the professional success and skills of the thousands of women both in and entering the legal profession, it is clear that the shift toward collaborative leadership will greatly assist women in moving quickly and successfully forward as leaders in the legal profession, in private firms, in corporations, and in government agencies.

Now, we explore contributing factors currently holding many women back and keeping them from reaching the top tier of leadership positions in the profession today. Although these barriers do exist, they are, in fact, artificial or contrived, as we will demonstrate.

Barriers to Women Achieving Leadership Roles in the Legal Profession

Women experience many artificial barriers to leadership in the legal profession. Many of those barriers are ingrained in the fabric of the daily work environment and society; however, in some cases they are imposed by women on themselves. The barriers identified through our research include:

- The "quicksand problem"
- The "Mommy Track"
- Compensation and business development structures
- Gender differences related to motivational factors
- Gender differences in communication

Quicksand Problem

Many women lawyers have proven to be effective at juggling conflicting demands on their time. Notwithstanding that skill, many women often demand perfection of themselves in every endeavor they undertake. Thus, if they think they cannot do a job to their own high level of expectation, they will not undertake it. Dr. Stephanie Pincus, M.D., a former senior-level executive of the Veterans Administration, calls this the "quicksand problem." The more a women struggles to be the perfect lawyer, the perfect mother, the perfect wife, the perfect daughter, and the perfect community supporter, when one or more of these endeavors is not performed at the level of expertise and perfection she demands of herself, she removes herself from the job that demands that she sacrifice time and quality on other fronts.

Women need to recognize the quicksand problem very early in their careers. They need to create a home life and allocation of familial duties that allows them to take on leadership responsibilities. Improving the leadership and delegation skills of women is an additional approach that can assist women in striking a sustainable balance between work and family that sacrifices neither their opportunities to obtain leadership positions in the field of law nor the needs and demands of their families. Women need to assert that they can be leaders in the legal profession. Then, and only then, will they be accorded the flexibility, both in their home lives and in their law firms, to lead in a manner that they determine is most effective to get the job done.

A key strategy for women to avoid the quicksand problem is to form support groups. These support groups, composed of both men and women, serve as an invaluable resource for mentoring, guidance, and advice. They also provide support and assistance in times of emergencies or great need. In addition to support groups, women can expedite their rise to leadership positions by writing articles, giving speeches, and taking a public stand that women with significant family responsibilities can and will be among the best people to become leaders in the legal profession and in their communities.

Mommy Track

We have observed that, unlike a majority of women, many men who aspire to or succeed in undertaking leadership roles in the legal profession create a shift in their lives to accommodate the increase in time and rigorous physical and intellectual demands that such roles require. Many men quickly downgrade in importance and effort their other roles (father, husband, son, community contributor, etc.). They pay less attention to these other endeavors early. That is made possible in part by the fact that society (both men and women) views men as having "lesser" responsibility for the family, community, and the home. The primary responsibility for the maintenance and well-being of the family, the home, and the community continues to fall disproportionately on women. These attitudes may slowly shift in time, but the near future does not suggest any rapid change.

This differential in the roles of men and women in the home, community, and family creates a challenging dynamic between men and women attorneys in a work environment. Some men, when they miss their child's birthday party or other important event because they had to be on a conference call or at a deposition, wear the sacrifice as a badge of honor, and it is viewed as such by many senior male attorneys. Implicitly, male-dominated law firms use this type of sacrifice as an example to be emulated by those who "want to get to the top." On the other hand, many women attorneys wear their failure to meet their children's needs as a badge of dishonor. This can lead to extreme guilt, unhappiness, decreased productivity and, finally, leaving the practice of law altogether.

Some efforts on the part of law firms to "accommodate women" have severely limited their leadership opportunities. Many firms have created a de facto "Mommy Track." By creating a "Mommy Track" these firms, intentionally or not, relegate mothers to second-class citizenship in the law firm or legal organization. Women "afforded" the Mommy Track universally earn lower financial rewards than their male counterparts (and former classmates) due to fewer billable hours. Frequently, the best mentors, clients, and matters in the firm or legal organization are systematically steered away from them. The result is almost always that women lawyers on the Mommy Track are rarely appointed to significant committees, which hampers or precludes their ability to become leaders in their firms. In many firms, the Mommy Track is also synonymous with being a "nonequity" partner. Often, when women take time to care for their children or families, it is interpreted as a lack of commitment and an abdication of their responsibilities to the firm, their clients, and the profession. Abdication is not a route to leadership in any endeavor, nor is it a voluntary decision to drop to second-class status within the firm or the profession.

The need of a woman to balance work and family priorities may require that leadership roles be delayed for a period of time. Keep in mind, however, that the needs of children and families differ. Leadership roles must not be permanently barred to women who cannot accept them while family demands are at their peak. A long-term view of the contributions that women can make to the legal profession over time is needed so that women who prefer not to have positions of leadership during their childbearing years will not be denied leadership responsibilities during their most professionally productive years, which may be in their 40s, 50s or 60s.

Being a caring, involved parent does not preclude leadership. Women need to mentor and be supportive of other women and men who have significant family responsibilities, and encourage them to undertake leadership roles and act as leaders for others with similar concerns. Creating an informal support system that goes beyond the office can make the difference between success and failure. In addition to its obvious practical benefit, it creates a sense of security that permits women with both home and client obligations to take on additional responsibilities that they may have forgone but for the knowledge that they had a safety net. If a woman knows that there are people she trusts to step in and assist her in an emergency, then she will be much more likely to undertake tasks that she would otherwise be reluctant to attempt. Strong, compassionate, collaborative leaders are needed to instruct others how to balance (or juggle) the multitude of demands placed upon women both inside and outside the legal profession.

Unfortunately, the stress and demand of balancing career and family has caused many casualties among our best and brightest women attorneys. The additional energy it takes to fight the system and create a workplace that is friendly to women undergoing dual careers of law and motherhood has caused many women to drop out. Any profession that consistently loses women because of "family demands" should assume that the family is not pulling these women away; rather, the work environment is driving them away. This is a waste of human capital that directly affects the bottom line. New perspectives and methods can result in changes in the culture and practices in the legal profession that are needed to promote the appropriate level of success for women. It is integral to the long-term success of the profession that increased meaningful participation by women in leadership positions be encouraged and supported in order to find real solutions to many of the problems women currently face.

Compensation

Another artificial barrier to women reaching leadership roles in law firms and legal organizations is the importance placed on aggregate billable hours. The business world is changing rapidly. Old expectations have gone by the wayside. Clients have embraced the flexibility made possible by technology. Using technology so that it becomes a benefit rather than a burden through effective leadership is best demonstrated by those who understand that every minute is valuable. It takes leadership to eliminate unnecessary meetings, conference calls, e-mails, and general busy work. Unfortunately, efficiency is not always highly regarded or rewarded in the legal profession. A conference call is most often billed on an hourly basis whether it was important or not. Some clients are trying to change this paradigm by placing "caps" on fees for single projects or paying flat-rate monthly retainers or project fees. Law firms with an emphasis on aggregate billable hours that are forced by clients to place caps on legal fees often decide to deploy cheaper, less-skilled subordinates to perform the work required by clients. While the total price may go down, the total number of hours devoted to a task or project remains the same or even increases. Experienced, efficient, highly skilled lawyers often lose out under this approach, as do clients.

Billable hours demanded of associates have risen dramatically over the past decade. The economics of the matter are simple and straightforward. The more hours per attorney billed and collected by the firm, the greater the firm's net revenues. The current norm in large metropolitan areas is 2,000 to 2,200 billable hours per year or more. In the 1970s, it was 1,600 to 1,800 hours. The current expectation of 2,000 or more billable hours works to the significant disadvantage of any attorney, man or woman, who has substantial responsibilities outside of the workplace. Again, this development has had a strong negative impact on women in the legal profession.

Women should be aware that the focus on billable hours represents an institutional form of discrimination against their achieving success and leadership roles. Other professions have found ways to reward efficiency and effectiveness over simple measures of billable hours or aggregate time. Money, power, and leadership are inextricably linked in our society. As long as the current system links billable hours to compensation and eventual leadership roles in the firm, attorneys who have family responsibilities are at a huge disadvantage, even when they are more efficient, more effective, and more productive than their counterparts.

The pressure for billable hours is less entrenched in government agencies and in-house counsel offices. Larger numbers of women have succeeded in these formats, but not at statistically representative levels. More research needs to be undertaken to find the root causes of why women are not at the forefront of these organizations in numbers proportionate to their skills and experience. There could be a myriad of reasons, including the fact that corporate transfers, reductions in force, and mergers take a higher toll on younger, less tenured employees, many of whom are female or who, as wives and mothers, have less flexibility to transfer from city to city to take advantage of the best career opportunities offered to lawyers in government or corporate offices.

Business Development

An additional artificial barrier preventing women from achieving leadership positions is client development strategies typically used in law firms. Traditional client development activities in the legal profession discriminate against women. It may not be intentional, but it clearly and systematically discriminates in several key ways. First, bringing in the client is deemed more important than keeping the client in many compensation formulas used by law firm. The compensation systems in private firms reward the "rainmaker" more than the lead attorney who does most of the work on the case. It is clear that bringing the client through the door is important, but keeping the client and doing excellent work for the client are equally important. A maxim of the real estate industry is that it is far more expensive to replace a tenant than it is to keep one. An analogous maxim applies in law, but most firms place far greater weight upon bringing in the client than on doing the good work to keep the client. Women often excel at creating supportive, long-term relationships of trust with clients. It takes time to achieve this, but once achieved, it is a bond that few clients are willing to or feel the necessity to break. Over several years, these relationships can become client generation vehicles as clients move from business to business or rise in the hierarchy in the business or client organization. If the firm structure is such that these long-term relationships are not valued or rewarded as much as bringing in the new client, then women will fall behind their more rapid-fire, client-generating male counterparts. This will continue to result in women leaving the profession or leaving a particular firm and finding other avenues or places for their time and talents.

Firms must recognize that many clients are loyal to the attorney and not the firm. If senior women associates or partners leave and go to other firms, the firm the female lawyer has left is at risk of losing clients. Poor retention of women lawyers, now the subject of a Third Annual Seminar by Hildebrandt, hurts the bottom line and reputation of the firm. In addition, losing clients at a rapid clip forces a firm to place even greater emphasis on obtaining new clients. This causes even greater detriment to the women who remain at the firm.

Another artificial client development and professional development barrier women face is that traditional out-of-the-office networking and client development activities used by (and paid for handsomely by) law firms to generate new business. These activities are designed, consciously or unconsciously, *by* men *for* men, giving them a huge institutional advantage over women in the firm. Many women, due to family commitments, cannot afford the time it takes to play golf or attend professional sporting events paid for by law firms to help attorneys obtain new clients. Some women simply do not have the background or interest in sports or golf to bring a meaningful level of banter to the sports-oriented event to be effective at client generation in these venues. Over time, the legal profession must realize that being a leader in the profession should not require that women take up golf or become knowledgeable about professional sports unless they are so inclined.

To address the bias in client development activities, senior women attorneys at several firms around the country have created women-oriented client development and networking events. The senior women partners in one firm embarked on this venture by inviting women clients, women business leaders, and women community leaders to a cocktail party, with the announced intention of providing a place where women could network with other women they may not otherwise encounter in their day-to-day careers. Law firms are uniquely situated to invite a broad audience to such an event, as their client base usually stretches across many professional areas. The initial event had approximately 50 women attending, including the women from the host law firm. Recently, one of their events had over 350 women attendees. From these events the firm learned that women leaders in the business community (the potential clients) are as strapped for time as women lawyers. Most women business leaders would prefer to spend an hour at a cocktail party networking than three to six hours at a golf course or professional sporting event with their lawyer or potential lawyer.

These types of client development networking events designed by women lawyers for women lawyers give women the opportunity to cultivate relationships that will create the longstanding client relationship they desire. As more and more women become leaders in business, the effectiveness of women as client developers will increase substantially. Short client development or networking events open the door for women attorneys to introduce themselves in a mutually comfortable, time-sensitive, and rewarding setting. These nontraditional forms of client development and networking need to be supported by law firms both financially and professionally to promote equality between women and men in seeking new business for the firm. Client development strategies and networking events and budgets that are clearly biased toward mega-sporting events not only discriminate against attorneys with substantial family responsibilities, they discriminate against women in the business community as well. This discrimination is now starting to be noticed by the legal profession, although it has been noticed by women in the legal profession for decades. In the long run, the firms that are creative in designing and supporting client development and networking events that work well for each gender on an equal, fair basis will have the most effective women lawyer retention and acquisition strategies.

When firms require specific amounts of new-client generation by attorneys who are trying to balance the demands of their profession with the demands of a young family, those attorneys with significant family responsibilities will either be shuttled into lesser positions or leave the firm out of frustration. It may well take women attorneys longer to generate business. Firms need to be patient in this regard, and not further handicap women by removing them from consideration for leadership positions simply because their client generation results do not match those of young male associates or junior partners. Given time and support, the financial benefit to the firm from client retention and generation by women can be dramatic and substantial. Firms that are shortsighted will not only lose the legal talents of women attorneys but will lose some of their client base, as excellent women attorneys leave to join more gender-friendly and progressive law firms.

Motivation and Communication

Removing artificial barriers in compensation, client development practices, and leadership requires an understanding of some of the gender-based differences in what motivates men and women and how they communicate. Often, for competitive men, their income becomes the measure of their accomplishments against others, which, in turn, is directly related to their self-esteem and workplace satisfaction. Men in many law firms are very aware of what their peers make and how many hours each bills and collects. For a majority of women, studies indicate that income is a factor but not the sole determinant of their self-worth, nor is it the strongest component of workplace satisfaction. Women lawyers report that they work for a variety of reasons, including intellectual stimulation, income, a desire to help others, and a sense of achievement.

In addition, men, to a much greater extent than women in the legal profession, have a well-defined and accepted culture of self-promotion. Gender-based expectations of society do not penalize men for aggressively acting in their own self-interest. Conversely, both in society and in the legal profession, many women who act aggressively in their own self-interest often become suspect, and are neither trusted nor well regarded by their peers and their superiors. This double standard may not be intentional or conscious. For that reason, it will likely be hard to dislodge in the legal profession or in society as a whole.

The positive effects of seeking and receiving acknowledgment and recognition in leadership development have been the subject of recent studies that are applicable to the current fate of women in the legal profession today. The book *Necessary Dreams*, by Dr. Anna Fels, a psychiatrist, makes the cogent argument that acknowledgment and recognition are essential sources of energy that propel people to become and remain leaders. Dr. Fels suggests that by minimizing their own accomplishments and failing to seek recognition, acknowledgment, and rewards aggressively for their accomplishments, women are cutting off their energy and ability to achieve leadership positions and succeed in those positions over the long run.

Women in most societies, including our own, often tend to downplay their achievements. "Smart" girls are taught that they can succeed in school and still be "nice" (read modest, sweet, humble, and feminine). The competitive legal and business worlds do not reward humble or sweet behavior or personalities. Women professionals are constantly torn between showing humility and showcasing their own accomplishments. In an ideal world they expect their peers and colleagues to know and acknowledge their achievements and reward them appropriately and fairly. It is not an ideal world. The disinclination of professional women in business and in law to promote themselves aggressively, combined with the negative reactions from their colleagues when they do, has had far-reaching negative

45

consequences. This includes a pattern of discrimination against women vying for leadership positions when they are reviewed by their male superiors in the legal profession for promotion or setting their compensation levels. This can be addressed by having both genders included in the leadership and compensation decision-making processes of the legal organization.

Conclusion

This chapter addresses key issues attendant to women, leadership, and the legal profession. It is one part of a national effort to bring the best that leadership literature and leadership development practices have to offer a profession that has a long history of leading the country with regard to issues of fairness and equality, but has not practiced those values relative to women in our own profession. The legal profession must adapt its own institutions and practices to maximize the contributions of all of its members. Neither men nor women in the legal profession can afford to permit differences in style, roles, communication, compensation, or client development strategies to continue to undermine the efforts of future women leaders to serve their clients, their law firms, their communities, their families, and our worthy profession.

CHAPTER 4

Ethics, Natural Law, and Leadership

"A life of values is central to professional satisfaction, and an extremely important way to live a such life of values is by providing leadership, not advice; to be the client, not just serve the client; to set the course as 'practical visionaries,' not just provide 'practical wisdom' about what the course might be."

Ben Heineman, Jr., "Lawyers as Leaders," Lecture,
November 26, 2006, Yale Law School

Lawyers and the entire legal profession have a special relationship with ethics. Because lawyers, judges, arbitrators, mediators, and many others in the profession occupy positions of great power and influence, ethics has been a mainstay of legal education, codes of professional responsibility, and a lawyer's or law firm's reputation for centuries. This chapter pays special tribute to the current and evolving role that ethics plays in the legal profession. Because there is no general theory of ethical leadership in the leadership literature, this chapter focuses on how ethics has evolved in the legal profession and how it can evolve in the future to support the desires of lawyers to be better leaders.

The ethical rules for lawyers are detailed, and teaching ethics to lawyers relies heavily on examples where lawyers were not ethical. Efforts to provide general ethical rules have been codified in legal texts for many decades. Yet many lawyers are looking for new ethical guidelines that can supplement the ethics courses they are required to take each year.

Many states require some education in ethics annually. The fifth edition of the *Annotated Model Rules of Professional Conduct* runs 721 pages.[1] The ABA has a standing committee on ethics and professional responsibility, and the first rule of the Model Rules after "Competence" is the "Allocation of Authority Between Client and Lawyer." Rule 1.2(a) is clear: ". . . a lawyer shall abide by a client's decisions concerning the objectives of the representation."[2] In two other instances, this rule uses the terms "shall abide by a client's decision." However, there is a huge caveat in this general rule, because the rule begins, "Subject to paragraphs (c) and (d) . . . ." Paragraph (c) goes to the issue of limiting representation if that limitation is "reasonable." Paragraph (d) states, "A lawyer shall not counsel a client to engage, or to assist a client, in conduct that the lawyer knows to be criminal or fraudulent . . . ."[3]

This rule sets the minimum standard of behavior or "platform" by which a lawyer must always abide without exception. The commentary is clear; lawyers must avoid "suggesting how the wrongdoing may be concealed."[4] Lawyers cannot even provide "passive assistance, such as withholding information from a court or government tribunal."[5] A lawyer may never advise a client to commit a criminal or fraudulent act.[6] No lawyer or any person in the legal profession is ever allowed to help a client pursue an unlawful objective or counsel unlawful behavior by lying or deceit.

Rule 2.1 of the Model Rules states, ". . . a lawyer shall exercise independent professional judgment and render candid advice. In rendering advice, a lawyer may refer not only to the laws but to other considerations such as moral, economic, social and political factors that may be relevant to the client's situation."[7] An important first question then is, what is meant by the term "exercise independent professional judgment"? Clearly, this term means the lawyer must abide by the ethical rules of our profession notwithstanding the client's objectives. Thus lawyers and legal professionals are never to serve merely as vehicles for achieving a client's wishes regardless of whether they are criminal or fraudulent. The commentary to the ethical rules of the legal profession is clear: "It is proper for a lawyer to refer to relevant moral and ethical considerations in giving advice."[8]

Where does the lawyer obtain information on these "moral and ethical considerations"? Not from law school. Not from continuing legal education.[9] A lawyer certainly gets this information on moral and ethical considerations from his or her upbringing, education, and daily life. However, unless and until such moral and ethical considerations are put into a lawyer's or law firm's platform, a client can never be certain that the advice based on moral and ethical considerations will be consistent over time from an individual lawyer, a law firm, or across law firms. Our section on natural law in this chapter provides strong answers as to where these moral and ethical foundations come from and how they are essential in the everyday practice of law.

The Model Rules even provide leadership guidance in the law firm setting. Rule 5.2 states, in effect, that a subordinate lawyer is not in violation of the rules of professional conduct if he or she does what a supervising lawyer tells him or her to do after the supervising lawyer has attempted to make a "reasonable resolution of an arguable question of professional duty."[10] This rule makes the more senior attorney totally accountable in this situation and limits the responsibility of the junior lawyer unless the junior lawyer knew that what he or she was doing violated the rules of professional conduct.

These rules related to supervision are needed to protect subordinate lawyers for several reasons. First, the ethical rules are particularly challenging for many junior lawyers. Second, the legal profession is strongly supportive of individual responsibility, and this set of rules clearly places individual responsibility for the acts of junior lawyers on the shoulders of the senior lawyers who gave them orders. Third, these rules implicitly acknowledge the reality that senior lawyers exercise "power over" (more than they exercise "power with") subordinate lawyers. The leadership style of most law firms and most organizations where lawyers work is hierarchical. Some law firms, government agencies, corporate legal departments, and other entities where lawyers work are beginning to use consultative leadership, participative leadership, and other forms of shared leadership. However, regardless of the legal setting, in the United States the "command and control" style of leadership is still predominant in these settings, and Rule 5.2 reflects that fact.

This chapter examines the emerging "ethics" of command and control forms of leadership. Rule 1.2 (abiding by the client's objectives) is designed to prevent lawyers from exercising command and control leadership over their clients. Rule 1.2(d) (no counsel for criminal conduct) is designed, as is Rule 2.1 (independent judgment), to keep the client from exercising command and control leadership over the lawyer. The essence of Rule 1.2 is that the lawyer can do nothing of a substantial nature affecting the rights of the client without the client's informed consent. This is the ultimate statement of participatory leadership and consultative leadership. Similarly, doctors are not able to make any medical decisions that substantially affect the well-being of a patient without informed consent expressly given by the patient (emergencies excepted). Thus, the bedrock, but often forgotten, leadership principle of both the medical and legal professions is the doctrine of *participatory leadership*.

Stated simply, both professions, legal and medical, hold that it is unethical to make a decision that affects a client's or patient's life without giving that client or patient a meaningful chance to participate in the decision-making process (again, emergencies excepted). This is the evolving standard in leadership development today.

For lawyers, the commentary to the Model Rules states, "Advice couched in narrow legal terms may be of little value to the client, especially where practical considerations, such as cost or effects on other people, are predominant. Purely technical advice, therefore, can sometimes be inadequate."[11] This passage should be read as a warning to lawyers that something very important might be missing from legal training and even legal experience. The section below on natural law strongly suggests that the literature and teachings of natural law represent an important element that fills this void in our current legal education and legal practice.

How does this new ethical approach affect the practice of law when lawyers are called upon to be leaders? This idea of participatory decision making will require more openness (inclusion) with clients and even with opposing counsel and adversaries. This new approach to leadership requires consultation and negotiation, rather than merely leveraging power to accomplish a client's ends.

There are still many law firms with more than 10 lawyers where one or two senior partners make all compensation decisions, all hiring and firing decisions, and most of the strategic decisions in client matters. Perhaps this was a good strategy a century ago. However, the improvement in the education of lawyers and clients, the broadening of young lawyers' desire to be meaningful participants in law firms' and legal organizations' governance, their strong ability to provide useful intelligence to aid decision makers, and their improved leadership skills all contribute to the growing convergence between the new leadership ethics espoused by this book and the new schools of management philosophy developing across the

51

United States. This new leadership ethic calls for greater in-clusion of lawyers at all levels in making key decisions, and for greater client involvement in the decisions that ultimately affect the strategy and approach used in pursuit of the client's goals. It also calls into question the basic validity of command and control leadership, which is still the predominant style of leadership practiced throughout the legal profession.

The teaching of leadership in legal organizations is also un-dergoing a transformation that will have a direct impact on law firms. In 2004, in a breakthrough training agreement, Reed Smith signed a large contract with the Wharton School at the University of Pennsylvania to teach members of the law firm leadership principles and skills. Although the provisions of the contract are confidential, the fact that the Wharton School was hired to teach Reed Smith's lawyers and key staff leadership development was publicly disclosed. To our knowledge, it was the first contract of its kind in which a law firm paid substan-tial sums to a noted leadership development organization to teach leadership skills to large numbers of lawyers and other staff in the firm. Although the results of the program are still unknown, the firm and those in the leadership development industry believe that Reed Smith will reap substantial competi-tive advantages from this investment in its lawyers and staff. Other law firms are now following in Reed Smith's footsteps with contracts with Harvard.

Natural Law: Leadership, Law, and Ethics in Tension

One thing all leaders have in common is followers. If lawyers want others to follow them, they must stand for principles that others hold dear. What principles do we as lawyers hold sa-cred, never to be negotiated or compromised? At the very root of our ability to lead is the ability to identify those principles. They must be important to society at large if we, as lawyers, are to attract followers. The collection of knowledge and principles known as "natural law" help form the basis for many lawyers who want to be leaders to identify, adopt, and promote a consistent base of principles upon which to base our claim to be leaders.

Law school applicants are screened to determine their ability to reason and to solve problems. They are trained to sharpen these skills. Their education and their practice nurture virtues like perseverance, communication, dedication, and competence. Their knowledge of the law gives them critical insight into the rules for interaction of all elements of society, information one might logically deduce to be essential in any public leadership role. This is the point Ben Heineman, Jr., makes in his recent lectures on lawyers as leaders. Heineman refers to lawyers developing the qualities of the mind that give them the broad perspective that puts lawyers in a unique position to exercise leadership.

Other chapters in this book focus on leadership competencies, leadership theory, leadership styles, and how our brain can greatly assist us in becoming better leaders. This chapter is different. It focuses on the foundation and principles of the legal profession and how to use these centuries-old precepts embedded in "natural law" to help promote successful leadership by lawyers.

Lawyers have *a major role* in society of dispensing and supporting justice. Natural law is the writings and knowledge gleaned from basic principles of justice, fairness, equality, and morality. Positive law, or the written law embodied in legal codes, judicial opinions, public policy, and precedents, is based on our everyday experience and our rules, codes, and decisions that judges and lawmakers make to apply legal codes and principles to everyday situations and to resolve conflicts and decide controversies.

Natural law and its principles are important for every lawyer who desires to be a leader, because during every lawyer's career there will be times when a strict application of a law will create, at least to many observers, an unjust result. Here is one example from a criminal defense attorney.

Two or three years out of law school, a lawyer had a criminal client who had been arrested for possession of heroin. He had been wounded in Vietnam and came home with an addiction that his trade as an electrician could not support financially. In representing him on the possession charge, the lawyer was able to suppress evidence based on constitutional arguments. The client walked free. There was another arrest and the evidence was again suppressed. Then there was a third arrest and the lawyer again had the evidence suppressed. Good lawyering? Principled lawyering? Did the lawyer have any other duty to the client besides keeping him out of jail? Positive law scholars would give the lawyer an "A+." Most people in society would not.

The lawyer knew he could not support his addiction on his income. The lawyer knew or should have known that the client was in need of treatment or he would become a threat to society. The lawyer in this situation came from the positivist school of law, and each time he got the defendant off, he felt he had done a better job than the last time.

The fourth time this client called the lawyer for assistance, he had been arrested for murder, having killed another man in a drug deal gone bad. A lawyer with the ability to combine principles from the school of natural law with training the lawyer received in the positivist legal tradition taught in law school would have figured out something the lawyer relying only on positivist law could not. He would have seen that his ability to get his client off criminal charges repeatedly was not helping the client lead a reasonable life. By acting only as a lawyer and not as a leader, the lawyer served his client only to a minimal extent, and utterly failed to serve society and its bedrock principles. The lawyer acting as a leader in that situation would have sought addiction treatment for his client (after one or more of the criminal charges were dismissed). A lawyer acting as a successful leader of a client in this situation might have prevented another human being from being murdered and the client spending the rest of his life in jail.

The "successful" defense of the client in the positivist school was ethical and, possibly, even brilliant. But the brilliant, successful, and "ethical" legal work done by the lawyer had significantly contributed to producing some negative consequences for society. The positive school, the criminal code, the lawyer's code of professional responsibility all forbade the lawyer, or at least did not require the lawyer, to weigh the interests of the community in making the judgments necessary to provide proper representation of the defendant. Positive law required only that the lawyer weigh the interest of the client and the formal requirements of the law. Yet we as lawyers are professionals entrusted with great privileges to assist society in reaching its most fundamental goals, life without violence toward fellow citizens and respect for the law. Each time the lawyer got the defendant off from the heroin charges without getting some help or assistance for his client's underlying problems, he jeopardized these fundamental values in society.

You can probably guess what happened to the lawyer in this case. He refused to take the fourth case, the murder case, and he stopped practicing criminal law. Soon thereafter, he began to teach law, leadership, and ethics so that the next generation of lawyers would always have the opportunity to learn fundamental principles from the natural law perspective rather than just learning positive law.

Non-lawyers and society at large cannot be expected to share the lawyers' reverence for precedence or legislative wisdom. They are more apt to relate to values like fairness, order, and justice. Leaders, in order to gain followers, must demonstrate key values held in high esteem by society. These values come from the writings and teachings we call "natural law."

What Are the Core Values of the Legal Profession?

There is the legendary story of Justice Holmes and Justice Cardozo having lunch. In saying their salutations, Justice

Cardozo said to Holmes, "Do justice," to which Justice Holmes replied, "Our job is not to do justice but to apply the law."

While this account is surely fictional, it seems to focus on one of the central tensions in the legal profession. When lawyers apply the law rigidly or use the law for their client's sole advantage, causing an unjust result, three things happen. First, when the lawyer's actions become known publicly, the rest of society holds the entire legal profession in low regard. Second, when one lawyer uses the strict application of a law, contract, rule of civil procedure, or regulation to cause injustice to another person, other lawyers lose faith in their profession, causing some to leave the profession entirely. Third, trust is violated, and when there is not trust in a profession or in some of its members, those in that profession will not be able to be effective leaders. In a recent meeting with executives from Volunteers of America, when asked to define leadership, one executive said, "trust."

Since the strict application of positive law can and will, on occasion, lead to injustice, relying only on positive law in guiding how we counsel and lead our clients can result not only in bad results for our clients, but it can squander the chance of our profession being viewed as trustworthy or as leaders of society.

Closely associated with the strict construction attitudes and long categorized as the *positive school* of judicial thought, this attitude that the courts should confine their work to enforcing the law as given by the lawmaking branches of government seems to be gaining a significant following in all three branches of government. Interpretation of statutes, according to this school of thought, should be a process of strict construction or, if one must go beyond the wording of a statute, the inquiry should be confined to divining the intent of the lawmakers. If application of this law in a particular case should cause injustice to a party, then such is the price we pay for law and order. In those cases where the law and justice are in conflict, the positivist school dictates that the judges and the lawyers must leave their conscience, and their principles of justice and fairness, behind.

By contrast, the *natural school* of judicial thought sees a much different leadership role for the judiciary, holding that the courts are primarily instruments of justice and that statutes and the Constitution are to be interpreted to effect justice. Accordingly, we as lawyers can know justice by reference to universal principles of natural law. Natural law theorists argue that notions of justice should guide not only the deliberations of legislators, but of lawyers who dispense "principled advice" to their clients. Clearly, justice is the duty of every branch of government and is the duty of each and every citizen, but it especially must be the calling of those in the legal profession who seek to be leaders.

This tension between the positivist school and the natural law school is not merely academic. It goes to the heart of how lawyers advise clients, how they represent clients, how our judicial process works, and its core values. The civil procedure professor at Georgetown University, Frank Flegal, in his closing remarks at the end of every civil procedure course, told his students, "What I have taught you will give you the ability to tie up any case for long periods of time, delay and deny justice, and it will give you the ability to promote justice. Do not use what I have taught you to deny or delay justice."

Natural law lies at the crossroads of disciplines as diverse as law, philosophy, ethics, sociology, and religion. We make the argument here that knowing the basic principles of natural law are necessary for lawyers to act consistently as leaders in society and in the legal profession. Lawyers are not merely technocrats, regardless of how technical our profession has become. Lawyers are not merely "yes" people bending to every client wish or demand, regardless of how rich and powerful some of our clients may be. As Ben Heineman, Jr., has often stated, a corporate general counsel's first duty is to be a guardian of a corporation's integrity and reputation. Guarding a reputation requires an understanding of how society at large will view a particular action. Lawyers, as leaders within our profession, and in leading others in other professions, must understand natural law sufficiently to be able to predict how others will react and view their actions. Earlier, we described the "psychodynamic theory of leadership" as the ability of leaders to anticipate how followers will view their actions, interpret their communications, and respond to their leadership overtures. Lawyers can obtain great guidance from the natural law principles of justice to develop keen awareness of the awesome responsibilities of being a guardian of an organization's integrity and reputation.

Natural law observes certain common principles. Chief among those are: 1) that there exists a higher law which is above man-made law; 2) that it is discoverable by human endeavor; 3) that it is universal in application; and 4) that all humans are duty-bound to act in accord with natural law regardless of the circumstances. With the birth of democracy in ancient Greece, notions of natural law emerged in tandem with the dispersion of power to citizens. Cicero, the great Roman statesman, seemed to capture the essence of the concept in this except from *The Republic III*:

> True law is right reason in agreement with nature; it is of universal application, unchanging and everlasting; it summons to duty by its commands, and averts from wrongdoing by its prohibitions.

The American Revolution was fueled by the conflict between the rule of law and natural law. The English King and Parliament relied on appointed judges to enforce the letter of the law on American colonials, justified only by the authority of their rule, completely disregarding natural principles of justice, which colonists held dear. The colonists argued that natural law was superior to the King's laws and that they could not be deprived of these natural rights.

Thomas Jefferson asserted in the Declaration of Independence that all men are created equal and *endowed by their creator* with certain inalienable rights, among which are life, liberty and the pursuit of happiness. Simply put, those who started America relied on the principle that the written law did not have a right to take away those rights that natural law provided to a citizenry.

Recognition of the natural law and action on that principle takes place at the individual level. It was not something to be outsourced to government or denied in practice by strict adherence to the written letter of the law. Natural law includes the principle that humans have a natural right to liberty, to be treated fairly and justly by others. In a sense, ethical inquiry is a grand effort to identify those universal principles of natural law. Ethical analysis requires that we independently analyze conflicting values and, using our own intellect, discover the natural laws that bind us and empower us as a distinct species. The premise is that humans are not just self-interested creatures but have another dimension that reveres outcomes like justice, fairness, liberty, and security. Both ethicists and religious leaders have pursued the definition of these higher laws.

Training in normative ethics is essential to all who aspire to know and recognize universal principles of justice. This is why we require the teaching of ethics in law school and have ethics exams as a prerequisite to becoming a lawyer. What is rarely taught or resolved in law school or bar prep courses is what a lawyer should do when there is a conflict between a man-made law and natural law. The same question can be asked another way, which will reveal the same answer. What should a leader do when there is a conflict between a man-made law and natural law?

Conflicts Between the Code and Natural Law

First, even to appreciate the existence of a conflict, a lawyer must know something about natural law. A domestic relations setting comes to mind. A mother and father are separated, but have filed no papers. They have a daughter who is now six. The father moves out of state, pays child support, but has not seen the child for two years. The mother lives with her mother, and the grandmother and two aunts take great care of the child. The daughter is doing well in school, has many cousins and a very good home setting. The father cannot provide a good home setting for the child. The mother dies suddenly. The father attends the funeral.

Man-made law says the father can take the child to his home out of state without even consulting with the grandmother or the aunts. Natural law says this would be a terrible result for the child, who has just lost her mother and is about to lose her entire support structure. Some state laws require the father to be judged a threat to the child for him to lose custody in the ensuing legal battle. Other states look to the natural law principle, "the best interests of the child," to guide the custody decision. In some states, grandmothers and aunts are considered second-class litigants with tremendous burdens of proof to obtain custody of a child against the natural father. In other states, all blood relatives are treated as equals in the court and "the best interests" of the child shall be the sole burden any blood relative must meet to be awarded custody.

While custody and parental rights laws generally allow the father to move the child to his residence in this situation, natural law and the best interests of the child standard would forbid such action. A lawyer who solely advises a client in this situation that he has full legal rights to take the child away at the funeral from her natural surroundings and the only support groups the daughter has known for the past two years is clearly not acting as a leader. Leaders take into account natural law principles of justice and understand the interests of all key stakeholders. Their decisions and principled advice is based on an analysis of what advice will produce the greatest good for all concerned in the long run, and is not limited to the narrow legal rights of their client when justice demands a result other than that which is allowable by law.

This is a clear example of how the principles of natural law stand head and shoulders above man-made law, and an example of how, when the two come into conflict, one should follow natural law and, if necessary, not enforce a man-made law that would lead to an unjust result.

In his opinion in *Wood v. Lucy, Lady Duff-Gordon* (1917), 222 N.Y. 88, 91, Justice Cardozo wrote: "The law has outgrown its primitive stage of formalism, when the precise word was the sovereign talisman and every slip was fatal." In *Jacob and Youngs v. Kent* (1921), 230 N.Y. 239, 242, he wrote that there must be no sacrifice of justice whatever may be the doubts of "those who think more of symmetry and logic in the development of legal rules than of practical application to the just attainment of a just result. . . ."

Leadership requires a lawyer taking into consideration both the written law and a well-developed sense of justice learned from a study of natural law when he or she gives advice and when a client seeks guidance. Lawyers who advise a client only as to the exact letter of the law are not acting in a leadership capacity, but as mere servants to the letter of the law. Just reading the statutes and cases is insufficient. Principled advice, the goal of every lawyer who seeks to be a leader, is best received and learned by the client, and best understood by opposing counsel, when the lawyer can communicate the exact principle that forms the basis of the advice. The goal of every leader is to offer the best possible counsel and for that advice be followed by clients, opposing counsel, opposing parties, judges, arbitrators, or any other party whom he or she wishes to influence.

Leadership has often been equated with influence. One of the goals of this chapter is to influence lawyers and law students to study natural law as well as positive law and to ground their advice in the best of both. By absorbing some of the wisdom developed over the ages in the field of natural law, lawyers add much to their intellectual arsenal that will support them as leaders. Lawyers whose advice advances the strong interests of society in justice, in treating all persons fairly, in promoting the common good, and in enhancing morality will have the best chance of developing a strong reputation as leaders.

Our legal system, from its inception, in the form of juries, actually allows for natural law, or justice, to trump the written letter of the law. The revolutionary leaders, legal scholars, and jurists in this country have debated for centuries whether jurors should be allowed to follow their own conscience in direct opposition to both positive law and instruction of the judge in a particular case. The trial of Peter Zenger is one of the most notable examples of the power of juries to return verdicts based on natural law in the face of persecutions based on the King's laws administered by the King's judges. Zenger was prosecuted for criticizing the King, and the jury was directed to bring in a special verdict deciding only whether Zenger had published the criticism. The judge insisted that truth of the criticism was not a defense and that the jury was to determine only the single issue of fact. Andrew Hamilton argued in Zenger's case:

> I know they (the jury) have the right, beyond all dispute, to determine both the law and the fact. . . . A proper confidence in the Court is commendable; but as the verdict will be yours, you ought to refer no part of your duty to the directions of others. (*Zenger*, 706, 719-20)

Peter Zenger's jury acquitted him in the face of both law and the judge directing them to do otherwise because they felt the King's law and the judge were unjust. The traditions of independent juries referencing natural law to find justice was ingrained in the early American system of justice and advocated by John Adams, Sir William Blackstone, Thomas Jefferson, Edmund Burke, Alexander Hamilton, and John Jay. Juries are allowed to follow their conscience to avoid a miscarriage of justice, providing a check on the power of legislators and judges.

The Requirement for Independent Judgment (Normative Ethics vs. Rule Ethics)

Lawyers who seek to be leaders in society and in the profession of law must know and communicate the written law and argue for its extensions and interpretations when those extensions and interpretations are necessary to achieve justice for clients and key stakeholders in a given situation. Lawyers must understand natural law so that they are sufficiently grounded in principle to realize how the written law must be extended, interpreted, or ultimately modified to promote justice and society's core values. It should be the goal of lawyers to become, through their advice and counsel, the instrument to bring into harmony the rule of law and natural justice. This is excellence in leadership.

Conclusion and Recommendation

Our culture is prone to see issues in terms of dualities: black and white, rich and poor, right and wrong, war and peace, good and evil, order and individualism, and winning and losing. If one can look beyond dualities to common ground shared by natural law and justice on the one hand and law and order on the other, lawyers who seek to be leaders can find ample opportunities to serve both the interests of community and individual responsibility. To see the two concepts as symbiotic rather than polarities presents the kind of possibilities envisioned by our founding fathers. Can we ever tell citizens serving on juries that they are to leave their sense of justice at home and apply blindly someone else's standard of justice when they serve? Should we encourage our judges to do likewise? Democracy, to be vigorous and to nurture the development of each citizen's human potential, must encourage the responsibility of each citizen to develop and live by an ethical standard as the core compass of his or her independent decision making. Should lawyers, judges, and jurors be advised to leave that at home when they function in the context of a judicial system?

Lawyers have shaped their skills and knowledge in our educational institutions, and for many, the effort expended (and the considerable debt incurred) is a necessary sacrifice they are willing to make because they want to help to serve and to change the world, and certainly to leave it a better place. That is the ultimate goal of leaders. The legal profession must be the place where society's ideals are enhanced and our sense of justice strengthened. The legal profession's commitment to justice must form the bedrock principle that is never negotiable, regardless of a client's goals. Leaders are always held, and hold themselves, accountable for the consequences of their actions. Lawyers who act as leaders must be willing to be held accountable for the consequences of their representation.

Studying the foundational values of our profession embodied in the field of natural law will pay substantial dividends to lawyers who seek to be better leaders. It will assist lawyers in becoming better grounded and respected as leaders, in giving principled advice, and to be more productive contributors to their organizations. In addition, knowing and deploying the basic tenets of natural law in their daily work will in all likelihood increase lawyers' levels of satisfaction. There is no guarantee that increasing one's knowledge and use of natural law in the profession will help a lawyer earn more money or accolades. It is our conclusion that it will help lawyers become better leaders.

Notes

1.   AMERICAN BAR ASSOCIATION, ANNOTATED MODEL RULES OF PROF'L CONDUCT, 5th ed. (Center for Prof'l Responsibility, 2002).

2.   *Id.* at 27.

3.   *Id.*

4.   *Id.* at 39.

5.   *Id.*

6.   *Id.*

7.   *Id.* at 289.

8.   *Id.*

9.   This author has found no course offered in law school called "Moral and Ethical Considerations," nor has he found such a course in his review of CLE programs. The author acknowledges that courses are offered on the biblical and Judaic sources of many of our laws in force today, but we find no primers in law school on morals. We are not suggesting that law schools should teach such courses. We are only showing the need that each person in the legal profession has to develop individual and organizational platforms based on moral and ethical considerations before lawyers can competently meet the test and requirements of Rule 2.1 and serve as leaders of leaders.

10.   MODEL RULES, 449.

11.   MODEL RULES, 289.

CHAPTER 5

The Value of Leadership Development in the Legal Profession

"Students come to law schools wanting to be leaders. However, the number of lawyers who are serving as leaders is declining."

Gregory H. Williams, *Teaching Leaders and Leadership*, ASSOCIATION OF AMERICAN LAW SCHOOLS Newsletter, April 1999

In 1999, Gregory Williams, the dean of the Ohio State University Law School, often implored law schools to teach leadership development. He wrote that "[e]mbracing leadership as a lifelong professional obligation will both enrich lawyers' personal satisfaction with their careers and serve our society. We must therefore form an alliance with lawyers and the bar associations to ensure that our graduates continue to develop their leadership potential even after they have left law school." Mr. Williams later became the 11th president of the City College of New York and served as president of the Association of American Law Schools.

If leadership development training merely answered Judge Barr's question (cited at the beginning of this book) and fulfilled the hopes of Gregory Williams by actually helping lawyers become better leaders and enriching their personal satisfaction, that would be enough to justify the expenditure of significant sums on leadership development training. But before we expect any law firm, legal organization, bar association, law school, or court system to spend money on leadership development, the rationale and evidence should clearly show why such programs and training will create tremendous value in the legal profession. Earlier we listed significant problems currently being experienced in the legal profession. Here we address each one of them again. Leadership development courses for lawyers can assist individual lawyers, firms, in-house counsel, and government employees with each of these challenges in some significant way.

High Rates of Dissatisfaction Among Young Attorneys

One recent book entirely devoted to this topic is *How Lawyers Lose Their Way: A Profession Fails Its Creative Minds*, by Jean Stefanic and Richard Delgado (Durham: Duke University Press, 2005). This book argues that formalism and the pursuit of profit at the expense of ethics is behind much of the dissatisfaction that is occurring among lawyers. These authors are persuasive that there is something terribly wrong in the legal profession today and, to quote the book, ". . . thousands more [lawyers] would benefit if their lives contained more leisure, more contemplation, more time to think seriously about what they do, and even enjoy it" (p.84). Further support for the thesis that lawyers are dissatisfied, and something can be done about it, can be found in law review articles such as "Why Lawyers Are Unhappy," by Martin E.P. Seligman, Paul R. Verkuil, and Terry H. Kang in 23 *Cardozo Law Review* 33 (2001).

Building on this detailed thesis that dissatisfaction is a significant problem in the legal profession, the role of leadership development courses becomes clearer as one of the means that may be usefully deployed to address this very high level of dissatisfaction among lawyers. Teaching and learning leadership development skills and aptitudes requires self-examination, introspection, getting to know oneself better, and becoming clearer regarding one's own goals and values. It requires getting out of the law office, away from the minute-by-minute pressures of client demands and hourly billing quotas. It requires not only studying leadership theory and practice, but also looking at biographies that show how others rose to leadership, found their calling, and learned to contribute to society in ways that empowered them.

The study of leadership development theory and practice by lawyers cannot guarantee great new insights, new approaches, and behaviors that generate lasting satisfaction among lawyers. Leadership development courses cannot, by themselves, ease the economic pressures that lawyers face and the challenges of dealing with clients with whom one may not agree or whose goals one cannot personally embrace. The study of leadership development can, however, guarantee the opening of new avenues to approach the daily grind of dealing with an adversary and can assist lawyers in finding new strategies to problem solving, creative team building, and the formation of win-win solutions. While no panacea, leadership development studies may very well be a good aspirin to a bad headache that too many lawyers face every day—chronic dissatisfaction with their professional lives as lawyers.

Poor Reputation of Lawyers Within Society

The American Bar Association commissioned a study of lawyers in 2001, and the number one conclusion from that study reported in *Litigation,* Winter 2001, Volume 28, Number 2, by Robert Clifford, Chair, Litigation Section, was that "[l]awyers have a poor reputation in American society. Americans say that lawyers are greedy, manipulative, and corrupt. Words like 'snakes' and 'sharks' were used by all of the groups in all of the markets tested." The report goes on to say:

Americans believe that the central place of lawyers in society enables them not only to manipulate the system but also to shape that very system.

Americans say that lawyers do a poor job of policing themselves. Bar associations are viewed not as protectors of the public but as clubs to protect lawyers.

Consumers are particularly frustrated with the fees lawyers charge for their services. They tell stories of lawyers who overcharge, are deceitful or coy about their fees, and won't account for the time they spend on a case.

Consumers also tell stories of lawyers who drag out cases to buttress their fees, misrepresent their qualifications, and exacerbate conflict.

This set of indictments against the legal profession is not often discussed in law school courses. Law students do not take courses of study to deal with the poor reputation of lawyers in society. Law students when they graduate are, therefore, unprepared to help reform and improve the reputation of the the profession they have chosen, since they are not given the skills to lead in the way that will be necessary to make even a dent in, much less totally transform, this horrendous reputational problem. The ABA report of 2001 stated, "Clearly, we must work to rebuild the public's trust in lawyering and to renew the respect society once held for its lawyers." Such an effort was actually started in 1978 by the ABA itself. It failed. And although the report concluded with the plea, ". . . we must first regain the respect and trust of the American people," no one to date has found any approach that appears to have merit in succeeding at this all important task.

This book makes the bold assertion that systematically taught leadership development courses can help the profession significantly improve the reputation of lawyers in society at large. Today, just as in 1978, lawyers do not have the skills to perform the leadership roles required of them. Also, lawyers today are not sufficiently focused on fixing their terrible reputation because they have become more technically oriented professionals who are less concerned with true leadership skills and aspirations. Leaders, by definition, care about and depend on their abilities to develop and maintain excellent reputations. Leadership development courses for lawyers would help lawyers place a greater emphasis on improving their reputation than any current CLE course now available in the marketplace.

Neither law school nor CLE courses teach lawyers the central role that reputation plays in a professional's overall level of effectiveness. The ABA report acknowledges this point explicitly when it states:

> In short, the poor reputation of lawyers in society is not just a matter of professional pride. It directly impacts the relationship that lawyers have with their clients and can even impact the public's willingness to use lawyers to solve their problems. It impacts the public's belief in the way the justice system works.

Therefore, lawyers and the legal profession as a whole are unable, after 30 years of concerted effort, to turn the reputation of lawyers around at all. In fact, since 1978, the reputation of lawyers has most certainly declined.

It must be presumed that the reputation of lawyers in the United States is not just a prejudice against a powerful group of people but is deeply rooted in the experiences that people and organizations have with lawyers every day. Stan Sorrell, the former co-chairman of the board and CEO of the Calvert Group, Inc., an investment company that pioneered socially responsible investing, used to refer to his legal department as the "sales prevention department" and disdained the multilawyer, multihour board meetings that cost thousands of dollars and were often convened to deal with minor technical points that could have been handled quickly and efficiently by anyone except lawyers.

Leadership development training programs are designed to help legal professionals improve in a key area where lawyers are notoriously bad and that hurts their reputation every day. Lawyers have a reputation for being terrible listeners. Active listening skills taught in leadership development courses throughout the United States would be a very positive development. Substantial improvements in this skill and other leadership skills would, in all likelihood, pay off in significant improvements in the reputation of lawyers.

High Departure Rate for Lawyers from the Legal Profession

In a recent article in *Forbes* magazine and posted at CareerJournal.com, a *Wall Street Journal* publication, Helen Lavan stated, "The number of lawyers who are dissatisfied and will drop out of active practice is growing." *Forbes* magazine reports that in California the number of inactive attorneys has risen by 50 percent from a decade ago. Further, *Forbes* says, a full 38 percent of attorneys say that they somewhat regret their career choice. Additionally, Harvard Law School counselors estimate that 20 percent to 30 percent of active attorneys are considering another career.

While no exact data could be located showing exactly how many lawyers have graduated from law school, passed a bar exam, and are no longer practicing, all of our research indicates that this number is staggering and should be a major concern to professional organizations of lawyers and to individual lawyers themselves. Again, leadership development training could provide a useful approach to dealing with this problem. First, leadership development training is designed to facilitate the best fit between one's personal goals and values and one's professional choices. Successful leadership, as taught in leadership development courses, requires true commitment to accomplishing what needs to be accomplished. This argues strongly for providing leadership development training to law students, since it can help them create and find a path where they can love what they do and find meaning in their profession. Too many students get out of law school and do not like the choices they have made for early jobs in the profession.

Through the study of leadership, lawyers might well find new ways to perform their work. Leadership development should be based on a careful analysis of why lawyers are so dissatisfied and are leaving the profession in great numbers. Such courses may well have the impact of stemming this tide.

Growing Economic Pressures on All Law Firms

No leadership development course can change the laws of economics. The growing wave of mergers of law firms reflects the need for larger revenues to cover the high fixed costs of providing high-end legal services to high-end clients. In addition, clients want "one-stop shopping" in legal services today, as there is a general view among corporate clients that the fewer law firms the company has to deal with, the better. Given the large-scale economic pressures on law firms of all levels, how can leadership development courses address this growing concern?

Leadership development courses and instruction can address this challenge, in part, through the teamwork modules inherent in most sophisticated leadership courses today. Successful leadership is the glue that can help merged law firms succeed and can help growing law firms integrate the ever-increasing number of lawyers and staff who work in law firms. Lawyers in large and small firms openly admit that their firms are "silos," with little interaction and even less real cooperative work being done by members of the firm in different sections.

While private-sector companies have found the advantages of "matrix operations" (where people from different departments work as groups on projects and report to supervisors from many different departments, rather than working in silos and always reporting to someone from their own department), law firms generally have not had the leadership development education and skills training to implement these complex operational structures. Leadership development courses can help law firms struggling with the bottom line understand more about the benefits of innovation, business planning, strategic planning, and the implementation of novel leadership and decision-making approaches in the law firm environment. Leadership development courses can improve the ability of the people in the firm to mentor junior associates, allow greater participation in decision making, and improve the decision-making ability of the organization as a whole.

The huge investment of companies in leadership development and the growing number of significant contracts signed by major law firms, such as Reed Smith with the Wharton Business School and DLA Piper Rudnick Gray Cary with Harvard University, all suggest that leadership development courses can offer some significant help to the legal profession as it faces ever greater economic pressures. In fact, the *Legal Week* article about DLA's conract with Harvard stated that it was a "groundbreaking move for the legal sector."

High Levels of Client Dissatisfaction, Formal Complaints, and Malpractice Actions

While this item is related to the poor reputation of lawyers, it is different in terms of how leadership development courses could provide some form of solution. As stated earlier, lawyers are often bad listeners, and this lack of listening skills gets them in trouble with clients. While usually technically proficient in oratory and communication skills, lawyers often fail to communicate with clients on a regular basis, fail to return phone calls, fail to consult with clients on tactics and strategies, fail to listen to and work with the client's real goals, and, most importantly, fail to satisfy their clients or serve them well. Leadership, and especially the concepts inherent in the area of servant leadership made popular by Robert Greenleaf (described along with 90 other brands of leadership in Appendix A), provide crucial learning tools for lawyers.

Leadership development training, and especially the leadership behavioral assessments that are often a component of these programs, can alert lawyers and law firms to areas where lawyers may have blind spots regarding their ability to work successfully with clients. Very rarely are lawyers sued by clients or admonished by bar associations for not knowing the technical aspects of the law. More often it is their limited client relationship skills that doom them and their clients to a less than perfect relationship and a bad result for the client.

Leadership development training courses can help a lawyer to see warning signs that things are not going well with the client early enough to take actions to avoid disaster. These courses will assist lawyers in better understanding their client's true goals and either meet them or part ways early enough in the relationship that no harm is caused for either the lawyer or the client.

The huge number of ethical complaints that the legal profession must process and decide must give great concern to those who ponder the future of the profession. Alternative approaches to teaching ethics, as provided by the leadership development literature and courses on leadership that have a strong ethical perspective, might prove to be a very strong complement to the unidimensional way that lawyers are taught ethics today.

Growing Levels of Associate Turnover

While this item is related to lawyers leaving the practice of law, from a leadership development perspective, it is quite different. Associates leave law firms for many reasons, and often the law firm management wants them to leave if they are not going to make partner. Leadership development programs can help promote and provide an environment where associates are given mentors in the firm who have been trained through leadership development courses to be successful. Research in the human resource literature shows that one of the most prevalent reasons why people leave their companies is they believe the quality of their manager is low.

75

By learning how to provide mentors to associates and by providing leadership training to associates, we anticipate that communication would flow much better between associates and other, more senior lawyers in the firm. We believe that if communication flows and mentoring activities were improved, associates would be less interested in finding another firm. Leadership development training can become a competitive advantage for law firms, as it reduces lawyer turnover and improves retention rates for those associates the firm wants to retain. In addition, leadership development courses will likely result in the law firm finding new ways to include associates in some of the governance practices of the firm. This will also help address associate retention challenges.

Prevalence of Outdated Governance Practices

It is beyond the scope of this book to provide a laundry list of outmoded governance practices that exist in many law firms. Many firms have one or two people making all key business and many of the professional legal decisions in the firm. Other firms may hold the compensation decisions of lawyers to a small management committee. Many firms encourage the creation of silos by giving lawyers completely free reign in their business development practices and in how they provide legal services. These management practices often result in a law firm providing a widely varying quality of legal services.

Leadership development programs can help senior management to develop more inclusive approaches to decision making, devise new ways to organize a firm's business development practices, and institute methods to make the compensation system meet the dual tests of rewarding business generation as well as professional excellence. Leadership development programs, if administered properly, can guide a law firm to innovative management approaches. By assisting law firms that use old-style, top-down management structures to develop more participatory management programs, the recruiting and retention of top-level associates and new partners will become easier, since these associates and partners will know from the first day on the job that their ideas regarding how the firm should be run will be taken into account.

The concept of "leader of leaders" is appropriate for the role of senior management of law firms today. Senior partners of large law firms must be able to steer the ship, and one cannot steer complex ships today without receiving excellent feedback from many different sources. One cannot steer complex ships either if one is a micromanager, trying to instruct each person working on the ship regarding each task they have to perform. Micromanagement was a viable leadership approach in simpler times. However, it is no longer appropriate for the top echelons of management in today's complex legal environment. Leadership development courses and training sessions can help show senior management of law firms how to refine their leadership skills. Such courses can show younger associates and new partners how to contribute in a positive manner to the improvement of the firm.

Continuing Evidence of a Glass Ceiling for Women

While the chapter on Women and Leadership addressed this issue in detail, there are two additional areas where leadership development programs could have a huge impact on helping women succeed to partnership or leadership positions in law firms, in corporate legal staffs, and in government agencies. First, such programs could give women the leadership skills and training they need to deal more successfully with the male leadership of other legal organizations. Second, leadership development programs could provide men in legal organizations with a new appreciation of the special challenges that women face in legal-oriented environments. This new understanding could lead men with the decision-making power in these organizations to better understand and appreciate the value of sharing power with women in the firm at earlier stages in their careers than they have been willing to in the past. The legal

77

profession is headed toward great difficulty if it cannot better integrate women into the leadership positions of its profession.

The loss of women lawyers from the profession is a serious blow both to the profession and to the women who feel forced out. It is a loss to clients who could benefit from their services. It is a loss to the firms that could benefit from their expertise. Leadership development courses and training could successfully address many of the challenges that women face in the legal profession in rising to the top of firms, corporate legal staffs, and government agencies.

Client Challenges to Increasingly Large Legal Bills and Insistence on Alternative Billing Structures

Leadership development and entrepreneurship are decidedly different subjects that require different teaching platforms. As an adjct professor who has taught courses in both subject areas, entrepreneurship and leadership development, I have found that there is much overlap in these two disciplines. Leadership development courses can assist participants in looking at the status quo as only one alternative to how the future might be. Leadership development courses are designed to open up the mind to pursue and embrace innovation. Such innovations in the creation of alternative billing structures may well be needed as the billable hour becomes more often the subject of client dissatisfaction and outright attack. Leadership development courses could also provide attorneys with training and better practices in communicating, at every stage of representation, their best estimates of the costs and benefits of each element of the representation.

Providing legal services is expensive, and no leadership development course can change this entirely. However, leadership development courses can assist lawyers in becoming better communicators with clients to show them why the expected cost of the representation is so high and can give lawyers a stronger willingness to master alternative billing structures that may provide a win-win solution for both the lawyer and the client.

Increasing Competition and Growing Use of Advertising to Obtain Clients/Business

There are many new marketing courses for lawyers. There is a new profession called "marketing director" for law firms. Advertising for lawyers has steadily increased throughout the United States each year over the past 20 years. In the past, lawyers obtained business by displaying their leadership and legal skills in client matters, in community organizations, and by writing insightful articles that showed technical and analytical mastery over an area of law, and they gave speeches throughout the community related to their civic and nonprofit-related volunteer efforts. Now, a 30-second ad puts a lawyer or law firm in front of millions of viewers, who apparently hire the lawyer or firm often enough to justify the advertising expense.

There will always be lawyer advertising. However, leadership development courses that promote the lawyer's ability to achieve great results for clients, that improve the lawyer's ability to achieve success in providing community and civic leadership, and in general help place the lawyer in a favorable light in the community may well be much more cost-effective than high-priced advertising. In spite of large-scale advertising, client development in the legal profession can still be very relationship-oriented, including "word of mouth" marketing we call referrals. Often, lawyers refer clients to other lawyers, without even asking for a referral fee. They do this based on the reputation of the lawyer and the exacting needs of a particular client for a specialist.

Leadership development courses, as explained previously, give a lawyer or law firm, a strategic advantage in obtaining and excelling in leadership activities in the community that can put lawyers and their reputations in a very favorable light with potential clients, with the media, and with other lawyers. In addition to just getting the name of the lawyer out in the community in a favorable way, the fruits of leadership development courses could allow lawyers to upgrade their client base.

In this era of increasing specialization among lawyers, enhancing the reputation of lawyers and law firms as a direct result of leadership development courses may well be the best business development strategy that will be available in the future.

Increasing Lack of Civility Among Lawyers

Entire books like *The Betrayed Profession: Lawyering at the End of the Twentieth Century,* by Sol M. Linowitz and Martin Mayer, have been devoted to the increasing lack of civility among lawyers. Even in Nova Scotia, the Barrister's Society has appointed a Task Force on Professional Civility. In 2001 the Illinois Supreme Court created a committee on professionalism designed to address the growing problem of lack of civility among lawyers in that state.

While leadership development courses cannot be the complete answer to improving civility in the legal profession, the perspective of respect for all parties inherent in leadership development courses would go far toward helping lawyers understand how being civil to other lawyers can benefit them, their clients, the reputation of lawyers, and the legal profession as a whole. Often lawyers will say they are not civil to other attorneys because other attorneys are not civit to them. This is precisely where leadership development teaching can play a huge role. The lawyers who say that they are not civil to other attorneys because the other attorneys are not civil to them are clearly acting as *followers* and letting the other attorney manage the tenor of the discourse, relationship, and conversation.

Leadership development courses instruct participants regarding how to manage conversations. They go to great lengths to teach participants how to at least manage your part of the conversation according to your standards and not the standards of others. The teaching of communication standards is a subtle but important. Leadership development courses would be of great benefit to the legal profession in improving civility among lawyers.

Increasing Delays in Litigation, Arbitrations, and Even Mediations

The litigation explosion of the last 40 years has created a huge backlog in our courts. Lawyers often find it in their client's interest to seek delay to avoid the day of reckoning.

Statements like "Justice delayed is justice denied" and "A denial of justice anywhere is a threat to justice everywhere" (Dr. Martin Luther King) are central tenets of leadership development books and courses. Leadership development courses teach people to look at the big picture and, while they would not teach anyone to sacrifice a client's legitimate interests in a matter, they teach people not to take advantage of situations just for the short-term gain of one person at the direct expense of another. The embedded concept of seeking "win-win" solutions, of using the rules the way they were intended and not just for delaying justice, and for making recommendations to clients that represent fair treatment to all even when the client does not want to hear such a recommendation, represents the hallmark of leadership development education as currently taught in the United States. Such teachings could have a significant impact on the huge backlog of client matters awaiting their day in court.

High Levels of Substance Abuse Among Lawyers

Another area where leadership development can play an important role in helping the legal profession deal with a serious problem is in the area of substance abuse. Due to the potential positive impacts discussed above, it is reasonable to believe that large-scale leadership development training can reduce some of the causes related to substance abuse among lawyers. In addition, leadership development courses are designed to assist people in taking action to help others deal directly with the problems they face. Too often, lawyers know of other lawyers who have substance-related challenges, yet do nothing, say nothing, and just let bad enough alone. Leadership development courses often propel individuals to take responsibility to a new level and approach others they suspect or know have substance- or alcohol-related problems. Back in 1988, Michael A. Bloom's article, "Lawyers and Alcoholism: Is It Time for a New Approach?" (61 TEMP. L. REV. 1409) documented the high incidence of alcoholism among lawyers. The American Bar Association has even produced a videotape, *Alcoholism and the Intervention Process,* focusing on a (fictional) alcohol-dependent judge. Many other articles and videotapes address this serious problem.

No leadership development course can cure an alcohol or substance addiction. However, when a lawyer is alcohol- or substance-"impaired," clients suffer immediately, and the legal profession as part of its self-policing function has a duty to take significant steps to protect the public from those lawyers who begin to fail their clients due to these problems. Leadership development courses could be one of the catalysts toward addressing a problem where little documented progress has been made over the past 30 years.

Dealing with Burnout and Lawyers Leaving the Profession

The number of lawyers who leave the profession is difficult to estimate nationally, and it is often asserted that women leave the profession in larger numbers than men. What we do know is that successful leaders are trained to recognize burnout and dissatisfaction among those whom they lead. The team theory of leadership states clearly that one of a leader's duties is to take care of his or her team members. To take proper care of a team, the leader knows, is to understand the needs of the team members. So often it appears that a lawyer quits a firm or even the profession in an instant, to the surprise of others in the firm. Usually, it is a result of a long process of dissatisfaction with the work the lawyer is doing or the work conditions. A keen observer and photograper, Ken Paul, has captured one huge challenge of the legal profession in a new trademark. The mark

82

is 25/8,® and to many lawyers it represents the workload they experience in the legal profession. Long hours are common to many professions, but being required to bill over 2,000 hours or, even in non-commercial legal organizations, to be expected to work seven days a week for long stretches is simply too much for many lawyers. Leadership training can help all lawyers recognize burnout in themselves and other lawyers and take steps well before a lawyer has decided to leave the profession.

Conclusion

These examples of how leadership development courses can begin to address some of the major challenges of the legal profession must at this stage be based on logic and inference, since lawyers have not taken leadership development courses in any great number. However, knowing the problems of the legal profession firsthand and being familiar with the teachings of the leadership development courses could yield substantial benefits to the legal profession.

CHAPTER 6

Leadership Assessment, Lawyers, and Legal Organizations

"The most successful leaders have a higher than average level of self-awareness."

Article by Julia Hayhoe, *Managing Partner* Magazine, Vol. 8, Issue 3, August 2005

One of the competencies that lawyers need to be effective leaders is a healthy dose of skepticism. We call it "constructive skepticism." Clients' memories fade, but their ability to convince themselves that they remember the facts perfectly does not. Opposing counsel feeds you information with great regularity that completely contradicts the facts as laid out by your client. Your own client, on occasion, changes his or her story, or cannot provide any evidence admissible in court confirming, or even suggesting, that his or her rendition of the facts is true. In biblical days, those who aspired to be judges in the courts were instructed to assume that each side in litigation was lying or mistaken. Only when the evidence was overwhelming that a particular side was telling the truth was the judge instructed to accept that version of the facts.

So, the first question anyone trained in the law should ask regarding leadership assessment is, is there any questionnaire that can give valid insight into how good a leader a person is? The short answer is no. Back in the 1940s, a world-class psychologist, Dr. John Flanagan, and colleagues informed the Navy that with the measurement of psychological responses during flights, they could accurately predict which Navy pilots would crash their planes. The Navy used this assessment tool to weed out these pilots and reduce the number of Navy air crashes significantly. This assessment led to the building of one of the great research institutions in the United States, The American Institutes for Research. Similarly, when AT&T was being deregulated in the 1980s, the company hired Dr. Michael Maccoby to do an assessment of 162 of its upper-level managers to determine if they could survive and function at a high level in the new entrepreneurial environment that deregulation was bringing forth. Dr. Maccoby conducted an assessment specifically designed for this query and determined that out of the 162, only three could do well in the new environment. Several years later, only three of these 162 managers were left in the organization, and two of the three were managers that Maccoby had predicted would succeed.

The state of leadership assessment tools can be summarized as follows. We can accurately quantify and describe the types of behaviors that persons are more likely to invoke in any given situation. The 40 leadership styles described below, which are attributable to the work of Somerville Partners, a leadership assessment firm, all lend themselves to being quantified through a series of questions that an individual can answer about himself or herself or that can be answered by others describing a person they know. When others answer questions about you, it is called 360-degree feedback, since these answers are most often collected from peers, subordinates, and managers. The correlation between the scores that subordinates, peers, and managers give and the scores that individuals give themselves is often very illuminating.

Knowing one's scores on these behavioral dimensions has four potential benefits that can help one to become a better leader. First, it can compare how a person scores in a certain behavioral area with how one's colleagues score that person. If there is a disconnect or great variance between one's self-score and the score given by others on the same behavioral dimension, it may shed some light on people's reactions to you in certain situations. Thus, leadership assessment tools can help in terms of improving one's self-awareness. While no mirror can answer the question, "Am I the fairest one in the land?," mirrors or honest, accurate feedback can give a lawyer substantial insights as to how he or she is perceived by colleagues or how he or she fits on the behavioral dimensions in a self-assessment situation. These assessments can suggest how one might strive to modify his or her behavior to avoid risks and challenges. Second, leadership assessments can pinpoint if a person is on the extreme of a behavioral dimension. While being on the extreme is not inherently negative in terms of how well a person leads, there is a great insight from the field of psychology that a "weakness is often an overdone strength." Showing a lawyer that he or she is on the extreme of a behavioral tendency can lead to clear suggestions on how to adopt new behaviors that may contribute to a more balanced and more successful style of leadership. Third, taking such a leadership assessment questionnaire and carefully studying the results can help focus the lawyer's mind on the question, "How can I become a better leader?" Certainly, focusing one's mind on this question can itself pay significant dividends in improving a lawyer's overall leadership ability. The fourth and possibly most important benefit of leadership assessment questionnaires is that in an organizational setting, be it a law firm, an in-house counsel situation, a nonprofit legal advocacy organization, a bar association, a government counsel office, or wherever lawyers work together, a leadership assessment survey can illuminate what we call "goodness of fit." Often, the quality of work performed in an organization is a function of whether those working in the organization are "on the same page" or aligned.

Lawyers are independent, highly educated people. Each has a unique approach to leadership. But legal organizations are led by senior lawyers, chairman and chairwomen, and managing partners, and when one's leadership style is radically different from that prevailing in the organization, work-related challenges can occur. It is very important to have solid data on the predominant style of leadership in all organizations where lawyers work. It is beneficial that this behavioral style be known by all in the organization. Where lawyers in the same legal organization have dramatically different leadership behavioral styles, knowing and understanding these different styles can help lawyers bridge the gap. Once they recognize these differences, people with different styles can either learn new ways to work together harmoniously or agree that it is time to part ways. Usually, knowing and understanding these different behavioral styles goes a long way toward improving working relationships, productivity, and workplace satisfaction and helping to avoid burnout, a significant problem among lawyers.

We are not arguing that "goodness of fit" in behavioral styles is a litmus test and all those whose scores are several standard deviations from the mean should be weeded out of the organization post haste. Quite the contrary. Learning the overall mean or average score on many of the behavioral indicators of everyone in the organization and comparing that score to the mean or average score of the high performers can quickly suggest what behaviors are more likely to lead to success, and the entire organization can begin to improve performance.

The goal of an organization answering leadership assessment questionnaires is to learn more about itself (self-awareness) and learn the differences in leadership styles. The conversations that result from entire organizations taking leadership assessments can be powerful drivers of people in respecting different behaviors and in being able to work together in a manner that improves individual performance, work satisfaction, mutual respect, and collective performance.

Until work on this book started, there was no leadership assessment in the public domain that was designed specifically by and for lawyers. One of the premises of this book is that leadership is best assessed, best taught, best learned, and best developed within a specific profession. The best leadership assessment tools and the best leadership development strategies for engineers, architects, doctors, lawyers, and other professionals should all be different. Each profession is unique, and the leadership behaviors and development techniques that are specifically designed for that profession will work better in that profession than programs that are designed for a general audience.

While it is beyond the scope of this chapter and this book to provide a full leadership assessment questionnaire and analyze its findings for each specific reader, we do provide six questions specifically designed for lawyers that will illuminate some of the behavioral tendencies most important to lawyers in the leadership arena. (A fully developed leadership assessment for those in the legal profession would comprise approximately 75 questions.) These questions cover two areas, problem solving and business development, which are generally considered very important to lawyers. In addition, based on how one answers each question, we provide some information about one's leadership style—its strengths and potential weaknesses. When a full-scale leadership assessment survey is taken, great care is taken to analyze not only each question individually, but how one answers all of the questions together. This complex analysis of the assessment forms the critical basis for determining a person's actual leadership behavioral style. The six questions presented in this chapter are designed to help illuminate one's leadership behavior on only a few of the 40 dimensions covered in a thorough leadership assessment. We have placed these six questions at www.leadershipforattorneys.com for those who prefer to work on an interactive Web site.

89

Lawyers work at a breakneck pace and rarely have time to reflect on how their own leadership style, behaviors, attitudes, and values may be contributing to their success or lack of success. If asked what are the actual leadership behavioral dimensions that psychologists have been able to decipher and quantify, lawyers and those in the legal profession might be hard-pressed to answer.

As we have emphasized repeatedly throughout this book, leadership, or becoming a better leader, can be learned. The 41 competencies we have listed in Exhibit 6-1 are certainly not the entire range of competencies that lawyers need to be successful leaders. They are the most important, however. These competencies are followed by 40 leadership behavioral styles in Exhibit 6-2 that reflect varying combinations of these competencies.

Exhibit 6-1
Competencies for Successful Leadership as a Lawyer

The competencies are:

1. Synthesize complex fact patterns
2. Active listening
3. Expertness in legal reasoning
4. Analyze historical information embedded in case law
5. Construction and analysis of legal codes and legislative intent (technical capability)
6. Persistence and resilience
7. Constructive skepticism
8. Organization of large bodies of information
9. Presentation and public communication skills
10. Interpersonal skills
11. Negotiation skills/proper estimation of real leverage
12. Empathy
13. Directness
14. Strategic thinking
15. Accountability
16. Conflict management
17. Client responsiveness
18. Problem solving
19. Integrity, a strong sense of ethics and reputation for integrity
20. Technological competence
21. Writing skills
22. Reading comprehension
23. Inquisitiveness/desire to learn
24. Precision in drafting and execution of client demands
25. Mentoring capability
26. Fairness

27. Intensity/ability to focus
28. Confidence
29. Intellectual rigor
30. Business skills
31. Able to predict responses to actions
32. Breadth of outlook to cover all ramifications of behavior
33. Creativity
34. Ability to build/work with and lead teams
35. Decisiveness and clarity
36. Open-mindedness
37. Ability to translate vision into reality
38. Desire and ability to acknowledge and respect others
39. Adaptability and flexibility
40. Ability to organize large sequences of tasks
41. Ability to document activities, information in an organized, retrievable manner

These competencies are needed in differing amounts in different situations. In many lines of legal work, creativity is essential. In other areas of legal practice, organizational capability of large bodies of information is more critical. Lawyers need to be able to recognize which particular competency is necessary for success on a legal matter.

The leadership styles listed in Exhibit 6-2 are more general and are designed to pinpoint key leadership attributes that are known to be correlated with leadership success. Becoming familiar with these styles will give you some insights about particular behaviors that leaders deploy successfully in given situations. From this analytical framework, we select six questions in Exhibit 6-3 to give you a sense of what a fully developed leadership assessment questionnaire might look like.

Exhibit 6-2
Leadership Behavioral Styles

Leadership Style Label	Leadership Style	Leadership Style Component
Strategic Driver	Strategic Drivers look for possibilities and formulate strategies for achieving them. They demonstrate a willingness to do whatever it takes, to outlast the competition, and to rise as high as their skills and abilities can take them. Strategic Drivers tailor their approaches to each individual, understand their impact on others, and demand excellence from their teams. They strive to make an impact on their organizations and readily take center stage in the endeavors.	Strategic Driver — High Conceiving, High Driving
Strategic Organizer	Strategic Organizers focus on doing the few things most critical to success while letting the other details take care of themselves. They develop concepts that guide action and employ imagination to overcome obstacles in ingenious ways; they readily break the rules when they become obsolete and base strategies on a comprehensive understanding of all the relevant issues involved. Strategic Organizers carefully plan for all contingencies and take the steps necessary to minimize risk. They insist on proceeding in an orderly and organized fashion, doing first things first within an environment characterized by stability and predictability.	Strategic Organizer — High Conceiving, High Structuring

Exhibit 6-2
Leadership Behavioral Styles (continued)

Leadership Style Label	Leadership Style	Leadership Style Component
Autonomous Strategist	Autonomous Strategists envision possibilities based on solid understanding of all the factors involved; display skeptical but logical critical-mindedness in examining what others observe or report; base most action on thorough analysis of objective data; pay attention to impact on others, tailoring approach to each person based on their perceived uniqueness; maintain emotional distance from others while requiring them to carryout their responsibilities.	Autonomous Strategist — High Conceiving, High Distancing
Strategic Formulator	Strategic Formulators work best from conceptual frameworks based on thorough understanding of all the factors involved; they prefer gathering information in a series of discussions with individuals whose perspectives they respect; prone to working with considerable autonomy, they consider all the possible negative outcomes that various courses of action might produce, but once selected, they persevere until objectives have been met; earning their trust takes time and effort, as they prefer keeping some distance between themselves and others.	Strategic Formulator — High Conceiving, High Contemplating

Exhibit 6-2
Leadership Behavioral Styles (continued)

Leadership Style Label	Leadership Style	Leadership Style Component
Strategic Collaborator	Strategic Collaborators develop conceptual frameworks for action based on understanding of the needs of people; they lay out the information in ways that allow people to come to their own conclusions; they establish balance between work and personal lives; they orchestrate action from behind the scenes, giving others their time in the spotlight; they involve people viewpoints in key decisions and avoid becoming too focused on single objectives.	Strategic Collaborator — High Conceiving, High Involving
Flexible Strategist	Flexible Strategists take complexity and formulate frameworks within which action takes place with flexibility and spontaneity; they develop a thorough understanding of all the factors in operation; they organize and plan the approaches to take in the moment; they demonstrate dedication to achieving the overarching objectives regardless of what it takes; they readily take calculated risks even under conditions of uncertainty.	Flexible Strategist — High Conceiving, High Adapting
Involved Strategizer	Involved Strategizers passionately commit to causes where articulating the best course is critical and where interdependency among members of the team is necessary for success. Involved Strategizers paint compelling pictures of where they want every-	Involved Strategizer — High Conceiving, High Engaging

Exhibit 6-2
Leadership Behavioral Styles (continued)

Leadership Style Label	Leadership Style	Leadership Style Component
Involved Strategizer (continued)	one to go while attending to the individual needs of teammates and protecting the best interests of the group. They involve everyone and incorporate the best ideas people bring into the strategy being executed; they encourage perseverance until success is achieved.	
Strategic Facilitator	Strategic Facilitators extrapolate complex information obtained from high levels of interaction with those having some stake in the outcome; with liberal use of imagination and understanding, they envision where things need to go and frameworks for effective planning; with energy and enthusiasm, they bring others into the efforts, invite contributions by a wide variety of people, and build affiliative and interdependent teams that get important things done; they treat people in ways that bring out their best.	Strategic Facilitator — High Conceiving, High Interacting
Collaborative Initiator	Collaborative Initiators take well-developed plans and processes and execute them with precision; require practical applications with minimal levels of theoretical or highly conceptual frameworks; need to balance work and personal lives and to keep options open; mix fun into work and require time to pursue recre-	Collaborative Initiator — High Involving, High Acting

Exhibit 6-2
Leadership Behavioral Styles (continued)

Leadership Style Label	Leadership Style	Leadership Style Component
Collaborative Initiator (continued)	ational activities; involve others and work in collaborative ways with people, put others in positions where they can shine; look out for the welfare of others and avoid conflict; encourage constructive criticism; lay out the facts and avoid one-on-one competition.	
Organized Collaborator	Organized Collaborators organize and structure what needs to be done and get an early start on things even without deadlines; they use methodical and systematic approaches to tasks while actively involving all those having a role; they give others opportunities to shine and create stable, predictable environments where balance between work and personal lives can be achieved; they infuse work with playfulness; they minimize risk, carefully examining all the possibilities before moving ahead.	Organized Collaborator — High Involving, High Structuring
Objective Collaborator	Objective Collaborators take a tough-love approach to people; they provide candid feedback, challenge assumptions, critically evaluate all information presented, and drill down to understand the underlying assumptions upon which proposed actions are based; they expect a lot from people but provide considerable support, collaborate with all those involved, and encourage others	Objective Collaborator — High Involving, High Distancing

97

Exhibit 6-2
Leadership Behavioral Styles (continued)

Leadership Style Label	Leadership Style	Leadership Style Component
Objective Collaborator (continued)	to move into the spotlight; they place value on establishing a balance between work and personal lives, allowing ample time for play; they keep their distance and control emotional expression.	
Collaborative Formulator	Collaborative Formulators foster environments characterized by minimal interpersonal conflict, solid balance between work and private lives, and high levels of mutual respect and admiration based on clear boundaries and respect for individual privacy. Collaborative Formulators provide objective observations based on independent thought and contemplation. They provide perspective, often identifying potential hazards in the roads chosen that others quickly come to respect.	Collaborative Formulator — High Involving, High Contemplating
Flexible Collaborator	Flexible Collaborators, in highly collaborative ways, see what needs to be done and take action, adapting quickly in response to emerging situations; encourage spontaneity and jumping on new opportunities without delay; remain open to new experiences and opportunities; thrive in situations where it is unclear what needs to be done and who has responsibility for what; involve	Flexible Collaborator — High Involving, High Adapting

Exhibit 6-2
Leadership Behavioral Styles (continued)

Leadership Style Label	Leadership Style	Leadership Style Component
Flexible Collaborator (continued)	others and encourage them to get involved and contribute; willingly take a back seat, enjoying seeing others excel; mix play and fun with work in an effort to maintain healthy balance.	
Collaborative Energizer	Collaborative Energizers actively engage people, providing energy, passion, and support; collaborate with those involved and place considerable importance on people's opinions and observations; they stay out of the spotlight while orchestrating activities and coordinating efforts; they treat people with compassion and understanding; they look out for the welfare of others and encourage balance between work and personal life; they reward loyalty and dedication, and they confide in and trust others without hesitation.	Collaborative Energizer — High Involving, High Engaging
Animated Collaborator	Animated Collaborators establish work environments characterized by cooperation, collaboration, optimism, and teamwork; they solicit and incorporate feedback of all sorts; they act as a resource for others and encourage people to examine the facts and come to their own conclusions; they openly share thoughts and	Animated Collaborator — High Involving, High Interacting

Exhibit 6-2
Leadership Behavioral Styles (continued)

Leadership Style Label	Leadership Style	Leadership Style Component
Animated Collaborator (continued)	feelings and pay attention to their impact on others; they encourage others to step into the spotlight; they keep their options open and maintain a balance between their work and personal lives.	
Flexible Opportunist	Flexible Opportunists demonstrate comfort with ambiguity, promote well-conceived change, and readily adapt to emerging events; they balance their free-wheeling style with an emphasis on taking the most practical and efficient paths to objectives; they attend to every detail, matching their experience-based templates for how things should be with what they see before them; they take calculated risks within areas where their expertise and experience lie; they eschew fancy or theoretical ideas and only take hold of those firmly grounded in reality; they treat people with consistency and play favorites with no one.	Flexible Opportunist — High Adapting, High Acting
Flexible Driver	Flexible Drivers are characterized by action. They rush into ambiguous situations, taking big risks, quickly adapting to emerging situations while organizing efforts in the moment. Flexible Drivers push for results and rely on those who achieve	Flexible Driver — High Adapting, High Driving

Exhibit 6-2
Leadership Behavioral Styles (continued)

Leadership Style Label	Leadership Style	Leadership Style Component
Flexible Driver (continued)	them without delay and with little need for support. Relatively indifferent to criticism, Flexible Drivers leap into the fray and drive others in ways that push for getting a lot done when there is little time left.	
Independent Adapter	Independent Adapters readily take on challenges characterized by ambiguity and risk, where logical and analytical approaches are required; they are quick to leap on new opportunities while downplaying any risks that may be present; they take a critical and questioning approach to understanding the circumstances and what needs to be done; Independent Adapters avoid being constrained by plans while being ready to change course when the time is right; they maintain emotional control even in the most distressing circumstances and keep relationships on a purely professional level.	Independent Adapter — High Adapting, High Distancing
Flexible Formulator	Flexible Formulators take calculated risks, think things through carefully after engaging in many one-on-one conversations; they anticipate all the ways things might go badly; once on a path, they demonstrate considerable resistance to influence by the	Flexible Formulator — High Adapting, High Contemplating

Exhibit 6-2
Leadership Behavioral Styles (continued)

Leadership Style Label	Leadership Style	Leadership Style Component
Flexible Formulator (continued)	views of others; Flexible Formulators readily make changes and adapt based on personal assessment of emerging events and changing circumstances.	
Engaged Adapter	Engaged Adapters take on ill-defined situations with ease; infuse energy and passion into every endeavor; they seek solutions that benefit the many relying primarily on observations and the views of others. Engaged Adapters are quick to make changes to plans and directions, putting the emphasis where the pressure is highest; they surround themselves with those committed to the same objectives, rewarding loyalty and commitment.	Engaged Adapter— High Adapting, High Engaging
Participative Adapter	Participative Adapters are characterized by their ability to involve others in achieving results in fast-paced, adaptive ways. They readily assume risks that give others pause; they quickly seize opportunities others take time to recognize. They enjoy bringing teams of people together to brainstorm new ideas and tackle new projects. They work well under pressure and become energized when challenging deadlines are present. Participative Adapters devote considerable energy and effort building and maintaining	Participative Adapter — High Adapting, High Interacting

Exhibit 6-2
Leadership Behavioral Styles (continued)

Leadership Style Label	Leadership Style	Leadership Style Component
Participative Adapter (continued)	networks of friends and associates and tend to have relationships that extend over along periods of time. They infuse others with enthusiasm and hope for what can be accomplished.	
Involved Activator	Involved Activators infuse enthusiasm and passion into all endeavors; invite participation in practical, action-oriented projects; reward loyalty and commitment; they attend to the details, take the most direct and efficient paths, and treat everyone with respect and equality; Involved Activators waste no time on theories or discussions about what needs to be done — they simply get something done in the least time possible.	Involved Activator — High Engaging, High Acting
Focused Driver	Focused Drivers push hard toward challenging objectives; involve others and take their inputs; drive toward success and beat any competition; they demand a lot from people but reward performance with support and increased responsibility; Focused Drivers take center stage; make a significant difference in organizations; cause people to change their views and align themselves with their agendas.	Focused Driver — High Engaging, High Driving

103

Exhibit 6-2
Leadership Behavioral Styles (continued)

Leadership Style Label	Leadership Style	Leadership Style Component
Structured Activator	Structured Activators take structured, methodical, and organized approaches to endeavors; foster thorough planning, anticipating all contingencies; they seek stable and predictable environments where only calculated risks are taken and everyone knows exactly what they need to do; Structured Activators infuse enthusiasm and compassion into projects, inviting the input of others and incorporating ideas and concerns into final plans.	Structured Activator — High Engaging, High Structuring
Engaged Formulator	Engaged Formulators demonstrate acceptance and compassion while holding their more intimate thoughts in reserve; they seek out and listen to the viewpoints of others and accommodate the needs of all involved while thinking things through for themselves; they take an independent and pessimistic view, exercising caution in the face of pressure to act; they surround themselves with those whom they trust and grant loyalty in return.	Engaged Formulator — High Engaging, High Contemplating
Engaged Participator	Engaged Participators readily show where their passion lies; they involve all those around them in determining what needs to be done; they look for noble causes to support and see the good that can come with little concern for potential downsides; they are	Engaged Participator — High Engaging, High Interacting

Exhibit 6-2
Leadership Behavioral Styles (continued)

Leadership Style Label	Leadership Style	Leadership Style Component
Engaged Participator (continued)	viewed as open books whose thoughts and concerns can easily be read by most; they connect to people naturally and maintain affiliations over the years.	
Energetic Socializer	Energetic Socializers see the bright side and are upbeat, enthusiastic and engaging; they maintain networks of friends, family and associates. Energetic Socializers involve others and set up interdependencies within teams; they seek practical, down-to-earth solutions and have no time for theories or ideas not based on experience; they waste no energy on lost causes, focus entirely on what's going on in the immediate environment, treat everyone as they want to be treated regardless of individual differences.	Energetic Socializer — High Interacting, High Acting
Participative Driver	Participative Drivers enlist others to participate in achieving things of importance; they are driven to make important differences and exhibit the single-mindedness of purpose to overcome most obstacles in their paths; they push people to higher levels of performance while exhibiting little patience for those unwilling or unable to pull their weight; their views of what's possible are	Participative Driver — High Interacting, High Driving

Exhibit 6-2
Leadership Behavioral Styles (continued)

Leadership Style Label	Leadership Style	Leadership Style Component
Participative Driver (continued)	compelling and filled with optimism for the future; they seek feedback but allow only a select few people to influence them once they have chosen their paths.	
Participative Organizer	Participative Organizers demonstrate a blend of optimism about the future with a desire for stability and caution about taking risks; they take methodical approaches to most challenges and encourage the development of well-thought-through plans and push to get an early start; they invite others' input and establish interdependent work groups with high levels of interaction and positive relationships.	Participative Organizer — High Interacting, High Structuring
Objective Participator	Objective Participators quietly get people involved and optimistic about what the future holds; they ask questions, show interest, and create opportunities for interaction and interdependency; they remain calm even in the face of crises; they objectively examine the information, apply logic, and arrive at conclusions based on the facts; they maintain professional distance from those with whom they are involved and set the expectation of high performance without the need for much support.	Objective Participator — High Interacting, High Distancing

Exhibit 6-2
Leadership Behavioral Styles (continued)

Leadership Style Label	Leadership Style	Leadership Style Component
Autonomous Driver	Autonomous Drivers seek center stage and strive to get things moving in directions that promise to bring success; they are stimulated by worthy competition, challenging objectives, and significant obstacles; they persuasively convince others to join in and push people to do their best; they have little patience with those requiring lots of support or encouragement — preferring, instead, those as driven to succeed as they are; they keep their emotions in check and logically and rationally think through decisions based on what the data and analysis tell them.	Autonomous Driver — Distancing, Driving
Objective Organizer	Objective Organizers make clear what needs to be accomplished; they carefully analyze all available information; they put things in proper order, doing first things first; they lay out plans, get early starts, and follow disciplined, structured methods to achieve their objectives; they keep emotions in check and maintain professional distance from co-workers; they prefer working with self-sufficient and independent people like themselves; they ensure that roles and responsibilities are clearly delineated and well understood.	Objective Organizer — Distancing-Structuring

Exhibit 6-2
Leadership Behavioral Styles (continued)

Leadership Style Label	Leadership Style	Leadership Style Component
Objective Contemplator	Objective Contemplators value their independence from the influences of others; they maintain professional distance from co-workers and value self-sufficient and highly competent people over those requiring lots of interaction and support; they critically evaluate information, question underlying assumptions, and pore over all the data, analyzing each facet; they carefully examine how alternative courses of action could go wrong and select the most reasonable one without displays of emotion.	Objective Contemplator —Distancing-Contemplating
Objective Actor	Objective Actors push for action; they ask challenging questions and objectively evaluate all information regardless of the source; they insist on taking the most practical and efficient course; they stay calm, cool and collected even during highly charged situations; they focus on the facts, attend to the smallest details, and determine the most logical paths to take; they attend to what's going on in the immediate environment, expect people to function with self-sufficiency, and treat people consistently regardless of their roles or personal issues.	Objective Actor — Distancing-Acting

Exhibit 6-2
Leadership Behavioral Styles (continued)

Leadership Style Label	Leadership Style	Leadership Style Component
Organized Driver	Organized Drivers take on challenging goals and systematically set about achieving them and beating the competition; they take center stage and persuasively enlist the support of others; working tirelessly, they plan each step to be taken in just the right ways to avoid unnecessary risk while ensuring a speedy exit should things go wrong; once the execution of a plan is initiated, they deflect criticism or contrary viewpoints of what should be done; they clarify roles and responsibilities and hold people accountable.	Organized Driver — Driving-Structuring
Contemplative Driver	Contemplative Drivers push to accomplish ever more difficult objectives and excel in the face of competition; they carefully and independently assess all available information; they use a keen sense of how things could go wrong to prepare for most contingencies; they work best with highly competent and self-reliant people who are as driven as they are; once they decide on a course of action, they resist attempts to influence them and pay little attention to criticism; they use persuasive arguments and dispassionate appeals to logic based on a thorough examination of all the factors involved to enlist others to participate.	Contemplative Driver — Driving-Contemplating

Exhibit 6-2
Leadership Behavioral Styles (continued)

Leadership Style Label	Leadership Style	Leadership Style Component
Action Driver	Action Drivers push to have a significant impact on their organizations; they seek the spotlight and opportunities to demonstrate their efficacy against worthy adversaries; they attend to detail and take the most practical approaches available to them; they waste no energy on lost causes and become impatient with those preferring to discuss what to do rather than doing it; they have little tolerance for people who can't or won't carry their own weight and try to treat everyone the way they want to be treated.	Action Driver — Driving-Acting
Organized Contemplator	Organized Contemplators plan actions carefully; they work to clarify roles and responsibilities and processes to be used; they take objectives and systematically follow defined processes to achieve them; they create environments for themselves that provide stability from day to day so they know what to expect; they communicate best using one-on-one conversations and take the time needed to observe and reflect on what they've seen; they take time to get to know people before confiding in them; they work best with considerable autonomy and independence, preferring to rely on their own resources whenever possible.	Organized Contemplator — Structuring-Contemplating

Exhibit 6-2
Leadership Behavioral Styles (continued)

Leadership Style Label	Leadership Style	Leadership Style Component
Action Organizer	Action Organizers quickly determine the most practical and realistic roads to take and set about putting everything in its place and getting things organized; they ensure roles and responsibilities are clearly defined; they look for well-defined processes and procedures to follow; they exercise caution where undertaking any new endeavors and prefer knowing what to expect with each new day; they search for how ideas or concepts can be applied before endorsing any of them; they get an early start on any new project and carefully plan each step; they treat others exactly as they wish to be treated.	Action Organizer — Structuring-Acting
Circumspect Actor	Circumspect Actors take the longer term view; they serve as the voice of reason when others are swept up in movements; they realistically examine every detail; they opt for the most practical and realistic approaches; they push for careful explanations of the applications that concepts and ideas offer; they work best with considerable autonomy, needing few outside resources; they take their time getting to know people, pay little attention to unsolicited criticism, and confide in only a select few; they associate with those necessary to be successful and waste little time or energy in pursuit of unachievable or impractical objectives.	Circumspect Actor — Contemplating-Acting

Exhibit 6-3
Assessing the Professional
Leadership Style for Lawyers

After reading the anchor statements above and below the numbered circles, indicate how well the statements describe you by darkening the circle that best represents your perceptions along the 1 to 10 point scales. "1" means that I am completely like the top statement and "10" means that I am completely like the bottom statement.

When I develop a plan of action for a client or for litigation, I focus my efforts primarily on asking probing questions to reveal enough details to assure myself that the plan has a high probability of success.

1   10

When I develop a plan of action for a client or for litigation, I push people to brainstorm possible barriers to success and then develop contingency plans to cope with every eventuality.

When I am involved with a client or my law firm/legal organization facing difficult decisions, I often articulate the alternatives along with the pros and cons of each to help our firm/legal organization or clients select the best choice.

1   10

When I am involved with a client or my law firm/legal organization facing difficult decisions, I ask questions designed to get them to think through the implications of various choices before moving to decisions.

Building a legal work environment where conflict is minimized and people treat each other with civility is critical to high performance.

1   10

Building a legal work environment that opens all sides of conflicts and disagreements to full and candid discussion is essential to constructive resolution and high performance.

Source: Somerville Partners

Exhibit 6-3
Assessing the Professional Leadership Style for Lawyers
(continued)

I have found that the best approach to obtaining new clients and cases is first to keep your eyes open for in-depth information about a potential new client that might suggest an opportunity. Once alerted, I have people gather information on the company or situation and any existing relationships. We then use those contacts to get meetings with various people and identify and define the opportunities.

I have found that the best approach to obtaining new clients and cases is to articulate and review our marketing strategy each week. We formulate and review plans for going after those clients we have targeted as most desirable and track our progress continuously. I resist getting our people distracted by opportunities that are not integral to our strategic success.

I have found that the best path to reach our revenue objectives involves expanding existing working relationships through the identification of new opportunities to provide additional value to our clients.

I have found that the path to reach our revenue objectives involves targeting prospects that meet our new client criteria where no working relationships yet exist and putting together a team to do the research and begin developing the kinds of relationships needed to win new business.

I am most gratified when I am recommended to other clients through my existing network of contacts. Instead of spending time researching future companies' needs, I am most successful working my network and establishing new relationships that lead to additional business.

I am most gratified by successfully targeting a prospective client where no strong relationships currently exist and executing a well thought-out strategy to get our feet in the door and close on important work.

Exhibit 6-3
Assessing the Professional Leadership Style for Lawyers (continued)

The first three items relate to problem-solving style with norm of 4.5.

The last three items relate to business development with norm of 3.36.

Level	Strong Type I	Moderate Type I	Slight Type I
Range	Less than 3.87	3.87 to 4.17	4.18 to 4.5
Problem Solving			
Range	Less than 2.21	2.21 to 2.78	2.79 to 3.36
Business Development			

Level	Slight Type II	Moderate Type II	Strong Type II
Range	4.5 to 4.82	4.82 to 5.13	More than 5.14
Problem Solving			
Range	3.37 to 3.94	3.95 to 4.52	More than 4.52
Business Development			

Type I Problem Solving		
Strong	**Moderate**	**Slight**
Goes to almost any length to maintain harmony while articulating various aspects of the issues; drills down into the details with penetrating questions until an in-depth understand-	Tries to steer people away from direct conflict and keep discussions objective and calm but tolerates some contentiousness; asks questions to get to the most important aspects of the	Tends to redirect discussions that result in conflict to less confrontational topics or points; prefers more objective consideration of the facts and issues but entertains subjec-

114

Exhibit 6-3
Assessing the Professional Leadership Style for Lawyers (continued)

Strong	Moderate	Slight
ing can be achieved; thoroughly thinks things through for him- or herself before laying out alternative courses of action along with the pros and cons associated with each of them; pushes to gain a quick consensus on the best path to take among the choices provided.	situation under discussion; after thinking things through, begins laying out options and initial ideas about possible advantages and disadvantages of each; influences people to adopt one but will consider those that others suggest as well.	tive viewpoints as well; does some preliminary probing for more details but is easily satisfied; presents a few ideas for how the issues could be addressed and one or two of the most salient pros and cons associated with each but invites others to add to them and provide more details or offer other alternatives.
Type II Problem Solving		
Strong	**Moderate**	**Slight**
Purposefully brings people into heated debates and direct conflict to draw out their best thinking; pushes people's thinking to identify all the viable options and potential consequences of each; poses questions that stimulate idea production and enhance chances of	Stimulates discussions and encourages tempered debates; points out the commonalities in opposing points of view and stimulates more in-depth analysis but sometimes provides solutions instead; guides discussions toward identifying potential root causes but sometimes	Encourages some open disagreement in looking at the issues and what may underlie them but keeps things from getting out of hand; after most people involved believe the causes have been identified, may elicit other opinions before shifting their attention to possible

115

Exhibit 6-3
Assessing the Professional Leadership Style for Lawyers
(continued)

arriving at the best possible solutions; pushes people's thinking in effort to anticipate how things could go wrong and what action could mitigate some of the undesired consequences.	suggests quick fixes instead; encourages people to develop some alternative courses of action and some of the contingencies to be considered, but on some occasions provides the answers.	solutions; draws out some alternatives and options and a few contingencies to plan for before moving on; usually moves things along fairly quickly; on occasion, may offer solutions instead of facilitating process.

Type I Business Development		
Strong	**Moderate**	**Slight**
Skillfully leverages existing network of clients and associates to identify new opportunities and build new business; quickly jumps on emerging opportunities as soon as they are detected; once identified, devotes the time necessary to research the issues and arrive for discussions extremely well prepared; leverages	Regularly taps into existing network of clients and associates to unveil potential business opportunities; once aware of new opportunities, follows up, does some research, and discusses the issues when appropriate; talks to members of networks regularly enough to unearth additional business opportunities; makes reasonable appeal to earn	Usually relies on information from established network of clients and associates to identify new opportunities but may target some prospects without first learning about potential opportunities; once opportunities are identified, completes enough research to have recommendations for prospect; regularly talks with

116

Exhibit 6-3
Assessing the Professional Leadership Style for Lawyers
(continued)

Strong	Moderate	Slight
business relationships to identify opportunities for persuading clients to engage in additional work.	new business from these efforts.	existing clients to find ways to do additional work or add value in new ways.

Type II Business Development		
Strong	**Moderate**	**Slight**
Takes strategic view of developing work; articulates desired types of business and criteria for classifying most desired prospective clients; targets qualified prospects and develops plans for approaching those meeting the criteria; develops approaches to prospects to enhance chances of getting a foot in the door; articulates compelling stories illustrating ways in which potential clients will be served that reflect the level of	Puts more effort into developing business development strategies than to leveraging existing client networks; uses a system of criteria to help target business development efforts but sometimes takes "'over the transom" work when it presents itself; in majority of cases, matches preconceived areas of expertise and experience with the types of business being pursued; takes the time to build some case stories that reflect the kinds of results that clients can realize	Prefers directing efforts at the right kind of business and clients but can follow more opportunistic courses of action as well; develops some criteria for classifying prospects according to fit with expertise and experience, but at other times follows leads provided from network; on occasion, references marketing plan to guide business development efforts but works outside of the plan when opportunities

Exhibit 6-3
Assessing the Professional Leadership Style for Lawyers
(continued)

Strong	Moderate	Slight
experience and expertise that will be mustered against the types of issues prospects face.	when expertise aligns well with the issues to be addressed.	present themselves; uses preconceived matches between experience and expertise and the type of work but also takes on work that is outside these parameters.

These questions are designed for individual assessments. There is also great value in using fully developed organizational leadership assessment tools for an entire organization, be it a law firm, nonprofit legal organization, in-house legal counsel department, a government general counsel's or district attorney's office, a court system, or other form of legal organization. The next section describes leadership assessment at the organizational level.

Organizational Assessments

Psychologists who study organizational cultures and behavior are well versed in knowing just how challenging it is for people to work together effectively if they have widely divergent leadership styles, or if they have a leadership style that is quite different from that of most of the other people in the organization. Now there is a new type of organizational assessment tool that not only seeks to describe the predominant behavioral styles in organizations, but has been designed to capture statistically reliable data on the drivers or predictors of future success of the organization.

In "Maximizing Your Return on People," in the March 2007 issue of *Harvard Business Review*, Dr. Laurie J. Bassi and Dan McMurrer show that the long-term success of organizations—whether schools, manufacturing companies, financial institutions, or chains of restaurants, and across every industry sector that has been studied—can be predicted by analyzing the responses from employees and hard data on the organization's past and current performance. While no study has been published using this new analytical framework on law firms, we believe that what has been shown to predict future long-term success in other sectors of the economy is equally applicable to the legal industry. In Exhibit 6-4, we provide 10 questions that have been proven to predict long-term success in organizations. To perform a comprehensive assessment that predicts future performance, a full 120-item questionnaire would need to be administered to every employee in the organization and the results would have to be analyzed.

The higher the score your legal organization achieves, the greater the likelihood of future success. On a scale of 1 to 10, a score of 1 or 2 on any dimension does not necessarily predict the failure or demise of an organization. However, such a score clearly indicates that the organization will have many missed opportunities, will have many shortcomings that could be overcome, and will simply not realize anywhere near its productivity potential.

These questions yield strong, predictive insights. Since leaders are responsible for the future of their legal organizations, it is time that they know the elements of their organizational culture that are most responsible for driving and predicting the level of future success or failure (missed opportunities) in their organizations.

A total score of 80 or higher on these questions (when answered by all employees or by a significant sample of employees of an organization) shows that the legal organization can be confident that its leaders have created and are maintaining a workplace where people generally perform at or near their potential. A score of 61 to 79 shows that the leaders of the organization are failing to meet some very significant challenges, and there is substantial risk that the organization is often missing significant opportunities to succeed. Scores of 60 and below show that the leadership is failing to act in a manner consistent with the long-term success, or even viability, of the organization, and its long-term future is in significant peril.

Scores of 60 and below also show that there is significant risk that newly minted law students will either not want to join this legal organization or will leave just a few years after joining it. Scores below 60 on this type of organizational assessment reveal great risk that productivity, quality of work performance, employee engagement and satisfaction, and administration are very uneven in the organization.

Exhibit 6-4
Questions that Predict Long-term
Organizational Success

For each question, fill in one score at the right.

1. Leaders' communication is consistently open and honest.   **Score**

1 =   This statement does not apply to our organization   _____
      at all (Strongly Disagree)
2 =   This statement is almost never applicable to our   _____
      organization
3 =   This statement is only occasionally true in general   _____
      about our organization
4 =   This statement is applicable to our organization   _____
      less than 50% of the time
5 =   This statement is applicable to our organization   _____
      about 50% of the time (Somewhat Agree)
6 =   This statement is applicable to our organization   _____
      about 60% of the time
7 =   This statement is applicable to our organization   _____
      about 70% of the time
8 =   This statement is true in our organization about   _____
      80% of the time
9 =   This statement is almost always true in our   _____
      organization
10 = This statement is universally true and applicable   _____
      to our organization (Strongly Agree)

Notes:

_____

_____

_____

_____

_____

2. Leaders seek out and act upon input from employees.   **Score**

1 =   This statement does not apply to our organization   _____
      at all (Strongly Disagree)
2 =   This statement is almost never applicable to our   _____
      organization
3 =   This statement is only occasionally true in general   _____
      about our organization

Exhibit 6-4
Questions that Predict Long-term
Organizational Success (continued)

		Score
4 =	This statement is applicable to our organization less than 50% of the time	_____
5 =	This statement is applicable to our organization about 50% of the time (Somewhat Agree)	_____
6 =	This statement is applicable to our organization about 60% of the time	_____
7 =	This statement is applicable to our organization about 70% of the time	_____
8 =	This statement is true in our organization about 80% of the time	_____
9 =	This statement is almost always true in our organization	_____
10 =	This statement is universally true and applicable to our organization (Strongly Agree)	_____

Notes:

_____

_____

_____

_____

_____

3. The firm has an effective system for developing leaders and planning for a smooth succession of the organization's next generation of leadership.

Score

1 =	This statement does not apply to our organization at all (Strongly Disagree)	_____
2 =	This statement is almost never applicable to our organization	_____
3 =	This statement is only occasionally true in general about our organization	_____
4 =	This statement is applicable to our organization less than 50% of the time	_____
5 =	This statement is applicable to our organization about 50% of the time (Somewhat Agree)	_____
6 =	This statement is applicable to our organization about 60% of the time	_____

Exhibit 6-4
Questions that Predict Long-term
Organizational Success (continued)

	Score
7 = This statement is applicable to our organization about 70% of the time	_____
8 = This statement is true in our organization about 80% of the time	_____
9 = This statement is almost always true in our organization	_____
10 = This statement is universally true and applicable to our organization (Strongly Agree)	_____

Notes:

_____

_____

_____

_____

_____

4. Leaders in my organization consistently recognize the contribution of employees.   **Score**

	Score
1 = This statement does not apply to our organization at all (Strongly Disagree)	_____
2 = This statement is almost never applicable to our organization	_____
3 = This statement is only occasionally true in general about our organization	_____
4 = This statement is applicable to our organization less than 50% of the time	_____
5 = This statement is applicable to our organization about 50% of the time (Somewhat Agree)	_____
6 = This statement is applicable to our organization about 60% of the time	_____
7 = This statement is applicable to our organization about 70% of the time	_____
8 = This statement is true in our organization about 80% of the time	_____
9 = This statement is almost always true in our organization	_____
10 = This statement is universally true and applicable to our organization (Strongly Agree)	_____

123

Exhibit 6-4
Questions that Predict Long-term
Organizational Success (continued)

Notes:

_____

_____

_____

_____

_____

5. **The leaders of this organization exhibit**   **Score**
   principled and ethical behavior.

1 = This statement does not apply to our organization _____
    at all (Strongly Disagree)

2 = This statement is almost never applicable to our _____
    organization

3 = This statement is only occasionally true in _____
    general about our organization

4 = This statement is applicable to our organization _____
    less than 50% of the time

5 = This statement is applicable to our organization _____
    about 50% of the time (Somewhat Agree)

6 = This statement is applicable to our organization _____
    about 60% of the time

7 = This statement is applicable to our organization _____
    about 70% of the time

8 = This statement is true in our organization about _____
    80% of the time

9 = This statement is almost always true in our _____
    organization

10 = This statement is universally true and applicable _____
     to our organization (Strongly Agree)

Notes:

_____

_____

_____

_____

_____

Exhibit 6-4
Questions that Predict Long-term
Organizational Success (continued)

6. My organization makes meaningful contributions to the community.

Score

1 = This statement does not apply to our organization at all (Strongly Disagree) ———

2 = This statement is almost never applicable to our organization ———

3 = This statement is only occasionally true in general about our organization ———

4 = This statement is applicable to our organization less than 50% of the time ———

5 = This statement is applicable to our organization about 50% of the time (Somewhat Agree) ———

6 = This statement is applicable to our organization about 60% of the time ———

7 = This statement is applicable to our organization about 70% of the time ———

8 = This statement is true in our organization about 80% of the time ———

9 = This statement is almost always true in our organization ———

10 = This statement is universally true and applicable to our organization (Strongly Agree) ———

Notes:

_____

_____

_____

_____

_____

7. My organization focuses on creating great outcomes for our clients.

Score

1 = This statement does not apply to our organization at all (Strongly Disagree) _____

2 = This statement is almost never applicable to our organization _____

3 = This statement is only occasionally true in general about our organization _____

125

Exhibit 6-4
Questions that Predict Long-term
Organizational Success (continued)

Score

4 = This statement is applicable to our organization less than 50% of the time   _____

5 = This statement is applicable to our organization about 50% of the time (Somewhat Agree)   _____

6 = This statement is applicable to our organization about 60% of the time   _____

7 = This statement is applicable to our organization about 70% of the time   _____

8 = This statement is true in our organization about 80% of the time   _____

9 = This statement is almost always true in our organization   _____

10 = This statement is universally true and applicable to our organization (Strongly Agree)   _____

Notes:

_____

_____

_____

_____

_____

8. My organization values and devotes sufficient resources to providing opportunities for employees to develop and grow.   **Score**

1 = This statement does not apply to our organization at all (Strongly Disagree)   _____

2 = This statement is almost never applicable to our organization   _____

3 = This statement is only occasionally true in general about our organization   _____

4 = This statement is applicable to our organization less than 50% of the time   _____

5 = This statement is applicable to our organization about 50% of the time (Somewhat Agree)   _____

6 = This statement is applicable to our organization about 60% of the time   _____

7 = This statement is applicable to our organization about 70% of the time   _____

126

Exhibit 6-4
Questions that Predict Long-term
Organizational Success (continued)

	Score
8 = This statement is true in our organization about 80% of the time	_____
9 = This statement is almost always true in our organization	_____
10 = This statement is universally true and applicable to our organization (Strongly Agree)	_____

Notes:

_____

_____

_____

_____

_____

9. Leaders are open to and welcome new ideas about how to improve our organization's business and professional results.

Score

	Score
1 = This statement does not apply to our organization at all (Strongly Disagree)	_____
2 = This statement is almost never applicable to our organization	_____
3 = This statement is only occasionally true in general about our organization	_____
4 = This statement is applicable to our organization less than 50% of the time	_____
5 = This statement is applicable to our organization about 50% of the time (Somewhat Agree)	_____
6 = This statement is applicable to our organization about 60% of the time	_____
7 = This statement is applicable to our organization about 70% of the time	_____
8 = This statement is true in our organization about 80% of the time	_____
9 = This statement is almost always true in our organization	_____
10 = This statement is universally true and applicable to our organization (Strongly Agree)	_____

127

Exhibit 6-4
Questions that Predict Long-term
Organizational Success (continued)

Notes:

_____

_____

_____

_____

_____

10. Work is organized in a way that makes good use   **Score**
of employees' talents.

1 = This statement does not apply to our organization   _____
at all (Strongly Disagree)

2 = This statement is almost never applicable to our   _____
organization

3 = This statement is only occasionally true in   _____
general about our organization

4 = This statement is applicable to our organization   _____
less than 50% of the time

5 = This statement is applicable to our organization   _____
about 50% of the time (Somewhat Agree)

6 = This statement is applicable to our organization   _____
about 60% of the time

7 = This statement is applicable to our organization   _____
about 70% of the time

8 = This statement is true in our organization about   _____
80% of the time

9 = This statement is almost always true in our   _____
organization

10 = This statement is universally true and applicable   _____
to our organization (Strongly Agree)

Notes:

_____

_____

_____

_____

_____

TOTAL SCORE _____

A full-scale organizational assessment gathers information from every employee in a survey format on these 10 predictive factors plus an additional 60 other indicators. The analysis of the data collected breaks down the results so that each section, each partner or manager who has direct reports, each office, each grouping of lawyers (associates divided into first year, second year, etc., equity partners, non-equity partners, and other groupings) and each area of administration, including billing, filing, paralegals, research, outsourced research, and every other distinguishable area of the legal organization, can be studied so that weak areas as well as areas of strength can be scientifically detected. These organizational assessments, once the scores come in, are usually accompanied by reports that include fact-based recommendations on how to improve each area, plus a careful statistical analysis of how important each factor is in predicting that organization's future. It is that last element, statistically and precisely weighing each predictive factor as it relates to success measures of the organization (number of cases completed, revenues, number of new clients, earnings per employee, or whatever success means to that organization), that is often missing in organizational assessment work performed by typical vendors in the field.

Conclusion

Leadership assessment, at both the individual and the organizational level, can yield significant information and actionable insights for those in the legal community that leaders can use to improve their own leadership behaviors and the leadership culture, norms, and operations of their organizations. Such assessments have the added advantage of being inclusive. With everyone in a legal organization taking both an individual leadership assessment and organizational assessment survey, they learn about themselves and their organization and contribute to the organization knowing itself better through objective data on critical dimensions of success.

There are many leadership assessment tools, companies, organizations, and practices today. Leadership development has been estimated to be a $4 billion business annually in the United States alone. By embracing and using the best leadership assessment and development tools available in our economy, legal organizations and all organizations that employ a substantial number of lawyers would be well advised to investigate the potential value of these assessments to the future success of their organizations.

CHAPTER 7

Teaching Leadership in the Legal Profession: The New Model

"In my huge law firm, we don't have anyone who can mentor new associates."

Chairman of a Law Firm

It is easy to state that lawyers should learn more about leadership development and should improve their leadership skills in order to improve their success and satisfaction as lawyers and managers. It is much more difficult to prescribe exactly how to accomplish these goals. This chapter asks the question: How can legal organizations begin to learn and teach leadership skills and principles in a cost-effective manner and thus improve the leadership skills and aptitude of those at all levels of the profession?

The well-established leadership development profession stands ready to serve the legal community. Law firm management companies are getting into the fray with new programs to teach leadership development. Universities are vying for the new leadership development business they expect from law firms. Can a law firm administrator just go out and hire a university or leadership development firm to do the job? It is not that easy, and we believe this is one of the reasons why law firms are so reluctant to spend the large sums demanded for leadership development training.

Certainly bar associations can try to give seminars and continuing legal education programs led by leadership development specialists, and law firms and legal organizations can begin the process of investigating the costs and benefits of leadership and organizational assessments without huge expenditures.

This chapter explains how leadership is often taught in the "in-house setting" and provides a new paradigm that will be much more cost-effective and productive in law firms and for in-house counsel, agency or court settings. There will always be "executive coaching" that is designed to help an individual become a better leader and become more conscious of his or her own leadership strengths and weaknesses. There will always be "leadership assessment tools" that ask the respondent how he or she would react in certain situations and what he or she thinks about certain issues. These tools can be highly instructive.

This chapter takes two new and different approaches to the teaching of leadership.

Mentoring

The leadership development program outlined below for legal organizations places a huge responsibility on mentors. A mentoring program at your legal organization requires two different kinds of resources. First, there must be people who can serve as mentors. Actually, while it may appear there are no candidates in your own organization who have the skills, interest, time, and commitment to serve as mentors for others, there are many leadership development consultants who can serve in that role. Whether you should designate someone in your organization or hire someone from outside to be a mentor is up to management. However, a written job description and written goals are essential so that an internal or hired mentor will know what is expected of them. Also, the amount of time the mentor should spend with each mentee should also be specified in general terms.

Mentors are just as relevant for solo practitioners as they are for 1,000-lawyer legal organizations. The mentee must also have clearly specified written goals and a willingness to invest the time and energy to work with the mentor to get the most value for each dollar spent in the mentoring relationship. While mentoring in legal organizations is rare, we may be at the point in the legal profession where law students like George Gilbert, who wrote the student's preface, will ask a prospective legal employer, "Please describe the mentoring program you have in detail for new hires, and can I look at the background documents for your mentoring program?" In fact, I am familiar with one family that, when someone marries into the family, assigns a mentor from the family to answer all questions, link the new family member to other family members, and do everything possible to make the newly married person comfortable. Certainly legal organizations have exactly the same goals when a new associate, or any new employee, joins the company.

We understand that mentoring takes time, and the billable hour is all-pervasive in many law firms. However, the time devoted to a mentor/mentee relationship (for example, two hours a week) is likely to pay off handsomely in improved work satisfaction, lifelong learning, greater employee retention, greater teamwork, and better client service. Starting a mentoring program can be as simple as assigning a more senior person to one or more junior persons for one month, one quarter, one year or longer. Teaching leadership development in this manner is a cost-effective way of improving leadership in legal organizations.

Purchasing Leadership Development Services

The purchase of leadership training today usually follows a similar process. Only a few at the top of the organization receive this training, and they are not expected to train others in the organization. This approach is highly inefficient.

It would be much more efficient to create leadership development courses that law firms and legal organizations can pay for once, with only a portion of their employees taking the course. Those employees could then teach others much of the material and lessons they have learned. Then the improved leadership behaviors learned by the "early adopters" in the firm could replicate themselves within their organizations through organic growth.

This organic teaching model for leadership is uniquely suited to a professional services firm like a law firm. Here, when those in the firm who learn leadership development become individual mentors and classroom instructors, the teachings are handed down from generation to generation in the firm and from lawyer to lawyer and employee to employee. Such a process would not only be more efficient, it would also serve as a "glue," bonding teacher to learner (employee to employee) throughout the organization. This would reduce turnover and associate dissatisfaction; promote mentoring and greater collegiality; lessen competition among lawyers in the same firm; and help to break down silos that can occur across practice groups and across cities. This learning model would be much more cost-effective than traditional leadership development training.

Certainly, not every lawyer or staff member in a firm who takes a course in leadership development will become an effective teacher. Inevitably, some people who take leadership development courses will not be good students and will not change their leadership behaviors significantly. The instructional model where students become teachers of leadership development is well suited to the highly educated environment of law firms and legal organizations. By creating courses that eventually produce in-house leadership development instructors, legal organizations will have flexibility so that the lawyers and employees of the firm can properly juggle client demands, administration demands, and leadership training.

Content for a Leadership Development Training Program

Leadership courses should deliver the knowledge of leadership theory, current leadership styles or brands, and leadership behaviors so that particpants enrolled will be able to achieve the following learning objectives:

1. ***Define*** the terms and vocabulary of leadership.
2. ***Comprehend*** the meaning of leadership from many theoretical and practical perspectives.
3. ***Apply*** the knowledge base that has been developed in the field of leadership so that in real situations the students will be able to develop and implement the most appropriate leadership behavior for themselves and those they lead.
4. ***Analyze*** situations to know which type of leadership behavior will be most effective for each situation.
5. ***Synthesize*** all of the knowledge in the course on leadership so that those enrolled will develop confidence in their ability to lead and teach others to lead successfully.
6. ***Evaluate*** leadership acts so that those enrolled will know very quickly whether the leaders (either themselves or another leader) are being successful and how to improve their leadership behaviors.
7. ***Use*** experiential examples and exercises so people can observe the participants as they take on leadership challenges and will be able to give the participants honest feedback on how they performed when faced with leadership challenges.

The leadership development course should be both intellectual and vocational. Those enrolled in the course should be expected to begin demonstrating improved leadership behaviors immediately afterwards in their personal and professional lives.

The leadership development course should be designed to stimulate participants to become "learners" in the field of leadership, as well as teachers of leadership to others in the firm. The best type of leadership development course for lawyers must encourage those enrolled to continue independent leadership study, exercises, group discussions, rigorous self-assessment, and assessment of others' leadership behaviors.

The course should be designed to promote the willingness, eagerness, and interest of the participants in taking on greater leadership responsibilities than they would have been willing to do previously. Ultimately, it should enable participants to become teachers of leadership in a short period of time, since lawyers, judges, mediators, arbitrators, investigative staff, and legal staffs not only have to be advisors and counselors, but must be teachers as well.

Most people working in legal organizations already have had nearly 20 years of formal education. Traditional lecture formats will not be sufficient to teach leadership development to the legal profession. Courses on leadership development, as well as motivation, must be innovative and use advanced pedagogical techniques such as:

1. Role-playing and simulations of the leadership styles and brands outlined above and opportunities for honest feedback, second tries, and discussion of the improvements and shortcomings of the participants in private or in groups.
2. Visual diagrams of leadership theories, leadership brands, and leadership checklists in addition to text-based learning tools.

3. Group and individual exercises that encourage participants to increase their willingness to participate in leadership activities and reward them when they do.

4. Detailed examples showing how poor leadership behaviors can create disastrous results for clients, law firms, legal organizations, the public at large, and the individual lawyers and legal staffs involved.

5. Written assignments identifying the leadership behaviors of the best leaders with whom they have worked in the past; homework assignments; writing a memo on the particular leadership style or theory that most appeals to them.

6. An assessment of how the individual participant's leadership style and behaviors fit in or conflict with the organizational platform.

7. A rigorous feedback system where others in the organization work with the participant regularly to assess and comment upon improvements or the lack of improvement in leadership behaviors and aptitude.

8. Asking participants to create a Leadership Workbook or diary to write down changes in their leadership behaviors.

9. Asking participants to develop their own list of leadership "best practices" and share them on a regular basis with colleagues.

10. A scheduling system for lectures, group exercises, mentoring, etc., that employs rigor and discipline while at the same time recognizing the need for lawyers and legal staff to deal effectively with client demands and emergencies.

11. Creation of Leadership Groups that will work together on projects, with each person taking a turn at being the leader. Each group would generate a written report on "Leadership in Action: Lessons Learned and Results Achieved" to share with other participants.

12. Those participants who want to serve as future teachers of a leadership development course would work with the leadership development instructors to develop their own "teacher's guide" for later use.

These teaching methods and courses of study in the field of leadership development are innovative. They are rigorous and demanding. They are based on the premise that additional knowledge, aptitude, and skill in the area of leadership are fundamental prerequisites to improving one's leadership behaviors.

For those in the legal profession who want to take and create courses on motivation as well as leadership, there are several guidelines to share. Given the very high burnout rate among lawyers, a course in motivation theory and practice would be quite important.

One might reasonably ask whether this teaching of leadership development and motivation might create disharmony in legal workplaces. Put more bluntly, could it foster an employee revolution? For the reasons below, we believe that such courses are much more likely to create employee *evolution* rather than employee *revolution*.

Leadership has been previously defined in this book as *the creation and fulfillment of worthwhile opportunities by honorable means*. In other words, leadership is all about making a contribution. This definition applies to one's family, community, and in all institutions where we participate. Unfortunately, somewhere in the historical evolution of leadership theory and practice, people got off track, and leadership became reserved for the few, the elite. However, the clear evolutionary process unfolding before us is a clear shift from anointing only a small cadre for all leadership roles to focusing on how to get more people (including employees, lawyers, and staff) involved in the tasks that were previously called "leadership prerogatives."

This leadership evolution will provide an opportunity to train others in the legal profession to assume more responsibility for leading, teaching leadership behaviors, mentoring, improving services to the clients, and improving financial results and other measures of success for their organizations. A CEO once known for being notoriously narcissistic and who made every decision, took credit for everything that went right, blamed others for everything that went wrong, never listened to any advice from anyone, and treated people callously once received some serious leadership development coaching. He, frankly, was not very coachable. But after a few months, he had made some progress. He started an organizational meeting by saying that he had worked hard in his leadership development training and had learned something. He had learned that he "had to do everything himself, but [he] could not do it alone."

While this parable shows just how hard it is for some leaders to allow others to participate as equals, even this tyrant of a CEO began to realize that the quantity of leaders in his organization made a difference, and slowly but surely even this CEO was on his way to endorsing "distributed leadership." Young professionals, be they staff or lawyers in legal organizations, know distributed leadership. They have been leaders in their student organizations, in volunteer efforts, in their churches and synagogues, in their families, and in their academic classes. They know, in some small way, how to lead, and even though they may not know how to lead clients in complex matters, how to lead legal organizations in the new legal business environment, or know how to lead judges or administrative tribunals through an arduous trial, they know they want to be part of the leadership team and they want to participate in a meaningful way in the decisions that affect their lives both professionally and personally. They know they are capable of filling a position where they can be a leader of leaders, and they will not wait 10 years in any organization to be allowed to step up to the plate to lead in important situations. They view law school and the training they received for the positions they now hold in legal organizations as their apprentice time, and they want to be given substantial responsibility, opportunities to be trained as leaders, and a real chance to lead on projects that require the coordinated work of many people. The failure of a legal organization to provide leadership development training to its employees and the failure to allow a very broad range of employees to asesume leadership positions are sure ways to waste important talent—which these organizations can no longer afford to do.

From the Clients' Perspective

Similarly, legal clients want highly motivated, independent professionals who are customer- or client-oriented, punctual, and responsive, and who treat them with dignity and respect. They want legal professionals who have a strong platform that embodies a clear sense of moral and ethical considerations and learning, and they want their counsel and legal staffs to have integrity, be credible, and be totally proficient in their trade. They want leaders assigned to their matters.

Leadership training and motivation training are designed to enhance a broad range of areas of human development. People are not born leaders. The idea of the "self-made person" is not only a myth, it is as ludicrous as the story about Abraham Lincoln, who, it was once said, "was born in a log cabin that he built himself."

There is a new leadership calculus emerging in the world. That calculus, simply stated, is: "All other things being equal, the more people who participate in the leadership of an organization and make worthwhile contributions to that organization, the greater the output of the organization will be, the more efficient the organization will be, and the better the organization will perform."

This increased quantity of leadership (more people participating in the leadership of legal organizations) creates an increase in the quality of leadership. Recognition of this emerging truth in the legal profession will spur the training and improvement of leaders and leadership. We will see leadership development programs (like the new one at UC Hastings on

Leadership Development for Women) and opportunities in law firms grow from the few who are allowed to participate in leadership development to the many over the next decade. Information technology will certainly fuel this new emphasis to create, foster, and support leadership behaviors among those people, including lawyers, judges, and legal staffs, who are willing to devote the extra time and effort it takes to help lead and help make a worthwhile contribution to the profession.

The Business Case for Teaching Leadership to Those in the Legal Profession

For these reasons, there is also a strong business case that can be made for bar associations and other private continuing legal education providers to begin providing leadership development courses for lawyers right away. Although the leadership development literature and educational sectors have been booming over the past 10 years and entering into new discipline after new discipline, the legal sector of our economy has not invested in training its professionals in the leadership field to any great extent.

In approximately 35 states, state bar associations require lawyers to take between 10 and 15 hours of continuing legal education annually (or 30 or so hours over three years). Most of these courses involve particular technical aspects of the law, from "How to Take Depositions" to updates on the changes in the law in subject matter areas where many lawyers specialize and where general practitioners need these courses to stay up to date.

A strong business case can be made that bar associations and private continuing legal education providers should begin offering leadership development courses. Because lawyers are called upon to lead as an integral part of the professional services they provide to clients both for fees and on a *pro bono* basis, a course on leadership development for lawyers and others in the legal profession would be of critical importance to

141

the legal profession. Being a better leader is one of the skill improvement areas that will surely help lawyers improve the services they provide to their clients. Lawyers are also called upon to serve in leadership positions, as directors of companies, as general counsel, as head of a government agency or its legal staff. Leadership development training is specifically designed to help participants improve in the performance of their duties in these areas. Being a better, more reflective and knowledgeable leader, and receiving specific training in the area of leadership development, can open up new possibilities as their clients become aware they have completed leadership development courses. They will be called upon to provide broader advice, accept more leadership roles with their clients, and provide more leadership-oriented advice.

If leadership develop courses are properly marketed, lawyers will quickly grasp the benefits as they look at their desk and see the pile of leadership demands that await their attention and execution. In addition, lawyers know that their ability to secure and succeed in leadership positions is a strong and well-honored way to promote their law practices and their reputation in the legal and client communities. This type of course should assist lawyers both attain and succeed or even excel in leadership positions, making them more efficient as leaders as well as more effective. Lawyers will see the connection between taking this course and improving in the one key area that they often use to promote their practice and generate new business.

Thus, a strong business case can be made for CLE administrators to work with potential vendors to develop one or more courses on leadership development for lawyers. The risk of financial loss is small. The potential for financial gain is great. The potential for making a significant contribution to the professional development of lawyers, law firms, government agencies with large legal staffs, and in-house counsel situations, and helping them improve in a "core" (but not well articulated or understood) part of their practice or organizational develop-ment system, is also quite large.

Conclusion

This chapter has sought to explain how and why leadership development courses should be developed for lawyers and those who work in legal organizations. While much of the information is quite technical regarding how to construct such a course, the gist of the chapter is that now is the time for individuals and law firms to begin looking to purchase leadership development training, and now is the time for leadership development trainers to take a serious look at the legal profession as a great new opportunity to provide leadership develcpment services.

CHAPTER 8

The Future of Leadership Education in the Legal Profession

"Shifting the field of law requires a new kind of leadership."

Steve Denning, Senior Fellow,
James Burns Leadership Academy, University of Maryland

With law firms such as Reed Smith and DLA Piper Rudnick Gray Carey already signing large-scale contracts for leadership development training with Wharton and Harvard, some would say the future is already here. With Holmes, Roberts and Owens becoming the first law firm in the western United States to invest in leadership coaching for its lawyers, and with Colorado becoming one of the first states to approve a CLE course that teaches leadership for lawyers that is open to all lawyers in the United States, one could argue that the future of leadership education for lawyers is already spreading throughout the United States.

As shown in the previous chapter, a strong business case can be made for leadership development courses for the legal pro-

fession. Bar associations and state supreme courts have the ultimate power to accelerate the creation and delivery of such courses,
as they are instrumental in approving them for CLE credit. Today, we have CLE-approved courses in time management,
PowerPoint, and other subjects far more removed from basic lawyering and client service than leadership development.

The growing emergence of the field of leadership assessment
targeted to the legal profession may prove to be one of the great
catalysts that convinces lawyers and law schools that teaching
leadership development is important. Given the high correlations
between leadership assessment scores and typical measures of
success, one would not be surprised if the best predictor of success for lawers is not grade-point averages, but how well one
does on leadership assessment surveys. Should that be proven
over the next five years, law schools will surely give leadership
assessment surveys to their students and give them courses that
may improve their scores. Similarly, if high leadership assessment scores are positively correlated with lawyer retention or
making partner, then law firms will certainly invest in leadership
development courses.

When a director of CLE suggested to a law school dean that a
course be developed and included in the huge CLE program of
the school, the dean said, "No. CLE is about training people in
skills we can measure." We are certainly further along in measuring leadership attributes than we are in measuring anything
related to ethics. Once the measurement issue is more fully developed, there will be a much greater push by the legal profession to take leadership assessment surveys and courses designed
to improve the leadership skills, aptitudes, and talents of those in
the legal profession. Ultimately, many law firms will insist on
some evidence that leadership development courses will improve
their bottom line. There is significant evidence that the higher
the measures of organizational leadership, the greater the profits
in businesses, as shown in *Harvard Business Review,* March
2007, in the article "Maximizing Your Return on People." In fact,
the leadership practices scores of companies reviewed in this
article shows that not only were sales higher when leadership

practices were better, but stock prices also were relatively higher. Thus, for those for whom the bottom line is everything, there is mounting, published evidence that the way to make more money is to have better, measurable leadership practices in your organization. Since so much of the revenue-generation engine in the legal profession is based on the performance of people, or human capital, rather than financial capital or machinery, we would expect this predictive relationship between leadership practices levels and profit/revenue levels to be even stronger in the legal profession than it was in the manufacturing and other sectors of the economy.

If money is not your motivator, we have given you plenty of reasons why expanding leadership development training is the wave of the future in the legal profession. Some have argued that the legal profession should get behind the creation and development of such courses because they represent a strong, new, and innovative way to improve the reputation of lawyers, address the growing lack of civility, and address some of the major ills affecting our profession.

Other Barriers to Leadership Development Training for the Legal Profession

Of course, lawyers have always been free to enroll in leadership development courses in the past and have often chosen not to do so. As Tony Grundy, my co-author in *Breakthrough, Inc.: High Growth Strategies for Entrepreneurial Organizations* (Prentice Hall/Financial Times, 1999) cogently explained, much of the behavior in an industry can be explained by understanding the "industry mind-set." The industry mind-set of the legal profession has been that leadership development courses are not needed by lawyers, will not help lawyers be better lawyers, will not help firms be more profitable, will not help legal organizations function more productively, efficiently or smoothly, and will not address successfully any of the ills currently challenging the profession and all of us in it. However, it is fair to ask, where is the evidence for that proposition? Industry mind-sets are so pervasive that they are taken as gospel and rarely subjected to any challenge or rigorous evaluation.

The future of legal education must be based on a fair test of whether leadership development training for persons in the legal profession can help. You can define help on any dimension you like, but the only way to test this proposition with any scientific rigor is to start delivering high-quality courses and collect data to determine if these courses are having a positive impact on legal organizations, on those who work in the profession, on the reputation of lawyers, on customer satisfaction levels of clients, and any other measures one wants to use as a dependent variable— even revenues per lawyer in law firms. Logic and evidence suggest that it is a very good bet indeed that leadership development training, if widespread, will be very good for the legal profession. Books never win arguments; only people do, and generally, only leaders take these arguments to the decision makers and convince them that the argument should carry the day.

Conclusion

It is now time for individual lawyers and legal organizations to take the calculated risk that investing in leadership development education, mentoring, improving the leadership practices in their organizations, and including more people in leadership will pay off handsomely. We predict that when lawyers and legal organizations take leadership development courses in significant numbers, they will begin to have a significant competitive advantage over those in the legal profession who do not invest in leadership development training. When this competitive advantage begins to manifest itself, the majority of people in the legal profession will support the idea that leadership development will improve law firms and legal organizations, make for better workplace environments, enhance performance, improve retention levels, provide better financial results, and help to create healthier work environments. Then they will vote with their pocketbooks to invest in leadership development programs for lawyers and those in the legal profession. We believe this will be the single biggest development in the next 10 years in the legal profession.

As law firms and legal organizations begin to allow, encourage, and even demand that all of their employees, clients, vendors, and even adversaries step up as leaders, leadership development training will be implemented quickly. Human capital has evolved too far to expect employees in the legal profession to give their best when they are not allowed to lead and are forced to utilize only a small percentage of their skills, knowledge, and abilities in the workplace. Law firms and legal organizations will achieve the next burst in human and organizational productivity by tapping into their employees' full ability to contribute. This dramatic improvement will occur when leadership tasks and responsibilities can be designated to an extent that allows all employees the opportunity to deploy all of their talents and knowledge all of the time. This can only happen through significant leadership development programs.

As Larry Downs, author of *The Killer App,* suggested in the December 2004 *Harvard Business Review,* improved management [and leadership] skills will be the next "killer app" in the legal profession.[1] We have seen this evolution in leadership development courses already start in the worlds of business, education, psychology, engineering, and other professions. We see it in the flat organizations that comprise many of the innovative, productive high-tech and knowledge industry workplaces.

The challenge facing the legal profession today is to make this move from "leadership by the few" to "leadership by the many" pervasive and well supported in law firms and legal organizations. This book and the outlines for the leadership courses described here are a small step toward dealing with the admonition of Gabriella de Audrey, a great artist, musician, and co-founder of the Maryland State Opera Society, who said, "Don't put talent where it can't get out."

That should be an important goal of law firm administrators, law firm chairmen and chairwomen, judges, heads of legal organizations, solo practitioners, and educators in the field of law. A new day is dawning where a lawyer trained in leadership development will be a better lawyer than one not trained in leadership development. And firms and organizations that train their employees in the art of leadership development will have a decided advantage over those firms and organizations that stand by the old model of "senior partner knows best."

The legal profession needs significant breakthroughs in:

- improving its productivity
- improving its reputation
- improving its civility
- improving its ability to serve clients at a reasonable cost
- improving its employee retention and satisfaction
- improving its ability to reduce burnout
- reducing substance abuse among lawyers
- helping lawyers cope with stress
- increasing worker satisfaction
- increasing lawyer retention in the firm and in the profession
- reducing the number of complaints against lawyers

Leadership development training will not solve every challenge of the legal profession, but it is also not merely a little step on the right road, either. The evidence is becoming clear that it may well be a major leap on the right road to improving the profession for our practitioners, our clients, and society at large.

What will drive the demand for leadership development training in the legal profession in the United States is simple. It will be lawyers and others in the legal profession wanting to be better leaders. It all must start with that desire by the several million people in the legal profession to want to improve their leadership skills and abilities. Then there will be a demand that leadership development become an integral part of a law school curriculum, as Gregory Williams suggested in the last century, and that CLE programs award credit for leadership development.

Now it is up to you. Do you want to be a better leader? Do you think it will help you be a better lawyer or a better employee in a legal organization? Do you think it will help you run a more effective court system? Do you think it will help you pass a bar exam? When these become burning questions, the legal education marketplace will respond to your demands. It is ironic that it will take real leadership by members of the legal profession to get the profession to invest in leadership development training for its members.

This book is based on the premise that lawyers and persons who work in the legal profession are leaders, and if they were better leaders, they would have more satisfaction and provide better service to their clients and organizations. The fact that the ABA is willing to publish this book and the fact that leadership development courses for lawyers are popping up in many states is evidence that this premise is correct.

You now have the tools, approaches, theories, and insights into leadership development to become a better leader. That was the ultimate goal of this book. After you review the materials in the Appendix, there will be no better time to embark on the effort to become a better leader and to help others with whom you work to be better leaders as well. You and the legal profession as a whole will be better off for it.

Note

1. A "killer app" is a new technique or application that dramatically improves productivity and is rapidly adopted in a widespread manner in an industry or profession.

Ninety Brands of Leadership Defined and Explained

Approximately 90 brands of leadership are currently on the market. We have divided them into the following 16 categories:

1. Ethical Leadership
2. Bad/Dysfunctional Leadership
3. Single-Leader Focus
4. Interactive Focus
5. Follower Focus
6. Multileader Focus
7. New Challenge Orientation
8. Nontraditional Organization
9. Results Orientation
10. Leadership Development/Training
11. Situational Leadership
12. Team Orientation Leadership
13. Traditional Leadership Brands
14. Visionary Leadership

15. Holistic Follower Orientation
16. Holistic Leader Orientation

We believe these categories accurately describe and categorize the types of leadership brands being taught today.

Category 1
Ethical Leadership

Character-based leadership: Character-based leaders place the common good at the core of their goals, and their leadership demonstrates concern for the personal development of their followers. Successful character-based leadership improves productivity and decreases worker turnover, because followers sense that they are assets and not expenses. In turn, this improves customer service and the quality of products overall. This leadership style or brand combines principle-centered leadership's integrity with the servant leadership's foundational goal of helping others.

Conscious leadership: John Renesch, author of numerous books on business, coined the term "conscious leadership" to describe leadership that originates from an individual's inner moral sense. According to Renesch, the conscious leader intuitively knows right from wrong and leads from a moral compass instead of from a prescribed code. Such leaders are likely to spontaneously take the lead when they sense a leadership vacuum, regardless of their official position. Conscious leadership radiates outward from the individual and seeks to take into account the group consciousness of all people involved in a project.

Contributory leadership: This term denotes leaders whose purpose and actions are designed almost exclusively to contribute to improvement of an organization, the members of the organization, and society at large. Contributory leadership promotes the broad sharing of leadership tasks and decisions.

Ethical leadership: This brand of leadership, through the work of Jo Ann Ciulla, Ph.D., professor of leadership at the Jepson

School of Leadership of the University of Richmond, and others may someday develop into a full-blown theory of leadership. Ethical leadership is leadership that is guided by and accepts ethical constraints and does not accept the theory that the goal of leadership is to accomplish a result regardless of the means used to achieve it.

Inspired leadership: This brand of leadership focuses on individually based, ethical leadership. Jamie Walters of Ivy Sea claims, "This very notion of inspired leadership obviously carries with it a self-referencing connection to ethics, integrity, compassion, dignity, and other 'heart-centered' and spirit-derived reference points."

Servant leadership: The term "servant leader" was coined by Robert Greenleaf in his book, *Servant Leadership.* He describes servant leaders as those who begin with the desire to serve and then gradually develop the aspiration to lead others. Greenleaf contrasts servant leadership with his understanding that some people want to lead first, and only serve others as an ancillary objective. Thus, a spectrum exists where servant leaders and narcissistic leaders are two extremes. Ultimately, the difference in these two brands or types of leaders is whether the leader is more concerned with personal recognition and ego or with the personal growth and well-being of his or her followers and the community he or she serves. Servant leaders are inclusive; they want to serve their community and use their leadership skills and position to expand the leadership roles and capacities of those they serve. Often servant leaders do not hold formal leadership positions but lead with influence and encourage collaboration among their followers. Servant leaders emphasize and demonstrate how ethics is an integral part of leadership through the example they set for others.

Steward leadership: Peter Block and Katherine Tyler Scott, President, Trustee Leadership Development, have written several influential books on steward leadership. This brand of leadership says that leaders are responsible for making decisions about and managing the resources over which they have control or

155

influence. Steward leaders manage these resources ethically and solely in the interest of the people whose resources he or she is designated to manage. In the corporate world, steward leadership includes being a good leader of people, a good steward of products and services, and a leader of the community. It maintains that the power to lead originates from below and is exclusively for the benefit of others. This type of leadership also has strong religious connotations and specifically rejects exploiting power and leadership opportunities for the benefit of the leader.

Trustee leadership: This brand of leadership, popularized by Katherine Tyler Scott and others, is directed to boards of directors and describes how leaders balance the relationship between their self-interest and the good of their followers and community. Trustee leaders believe that their role as leaders is completely tied to the common good, and they try to integrate the personal aspects of being a leader with professional, individual, and community interests that grow out of their leadership actions. Trustee leadership can apply in the for-profit, nonprofit, political, and policy realms. James Kouzes, author of *The Leadership Challenges*, writes that "you cannot lead others until you have first led yourself through a struggle of opposing values." Trustee leaders both develop a vision and participate as trustees of the leadership position and status that others have conferred upon them.

Values-based leadership: This brand of leadership requires the leader to understand the different and sometimes contrasting ideas, values, and needs of those involved in a project or organization, and then articulate the moral and ethical values and principles upon which the leader bases his or her decisions and actions. People from Steve Jobs, the co-founder of Apple Computer, Inc., to General Norman Schwartzkopf claim that values-based leadership is most important in today's business world and in public life because people who care about similar values work best together and can build the bonds of trust required for successful leadership. Values-based leadership encourages trust and can be very helpful when building interpersonal relationships. Values-based leadership includes three key areas: effectiveness, morality, and a focus on long-term goals.

Values-centered leadership: William J. O'Brien has written extensively about this leadership approach in his book, *The Soul of Corporate Leadership: Guidelines for Value-Centered Governance.* This brand of leadership occurs when the values of the leader and the values of the followers are fused and become one, emanating from either direction. In such an atmosphere, followers are involved and motivated to help others and to be a part of something larger than themselves. Sam Walton, founder of Wal-Mart, mastered this leadership technique. The Wal-Mart training program teaches each trainee the personal values of the founder and subsequently the values of the corporation. Each follower is then expected to embrace these values not only at work, but also in his or her personal life. Ideally, this type of leadership creates an environment in which followers promote, demonstrate, and defend the organization's values.

Category 2
Bad/Dysfunctional Leadership

Bogus leadership: This is opposite of conscious leadership. Bogus leadership occurs when leaders follow a narrow or scripted type of leadership that does not reflect who they are. Their insistence on following a single leadership paradigm limits their thinking, giving them fewer options and causing them to act more slowly than conscious leaders, who lead from their moral compass and group consciousness.

Narcissistic leadership: This type of leadership occurs when leaders are motivated primarily by their desire to serve their egos. Generally, narcissistic leaders keep very high profiles. It should be clear that narcissistic leadership does not necessarily mean unproductive leadership. Michael Maccoby, author of *The Productive Narcissist: The Promise and Peril of Visionary Leaders*, argues that narcissistic leaders are generally useful in times of transition or turbulence because they have the personal popular-

157

ity and charisma to make massive changes. Over time, however, these leaders tend to become unrealistic dreamers, and their leadership styles can drag down their companies. Narcissistic leaders tend to ignore advice and take a top-down approach to leading. Narcissistic leaders are marked by great vision and many followers, who are often more personally loyal to the narcissistic leader than to his or her vision and policies. The weaknesses of narcissistic leaders include oversensitivity to criticism, lack of empathy, poor listening skills, distaste for mentoring, and an excessive desire to compete.

Reactive leadership: This leadership style or brand is the opposite of proactive leadership. Reactive leaders expect and assume the worst from their followers, sometimes treating them as if they were children. Reactive leaders tend to focus on weaknesses and negatives, rarely providing positive encouragement. Reactive leaders address issues only after they occur, instead of anticipating and handling future challenges. This creates an air of crisis, making the leader seem disorganized. To further complicate matters, reactive leaders are often unclear about their goals and lack a vision for the future. Because of these attributes, reactive leaders tend to punish employees after the fact rather than guide them toward a clear goal in advance.

Toxic leadership: This leadership style is also called "destructive leadership." It has been studied by Jean Lipman-Blumen in her book, *The Allure of Toxic Leaders: Why We Follow Destructive Bosses.* This brand of leadership harms an organization by focusing relentlessly on short-term goals. Toxic leadership ignores the morale of followers and their working conditions. Ultimately, toxic leaders can be identified by the long-term effects of their destructive behavior. Their followers perform poorly for several reasons. First, they often feel compelled to overfocus on the short term. Second, they are discouraged by the myopic focus on the bottom line and the poor choices inherent in their leadership style. Third, toxic leaders have poor interpersonal skills, which hurt the self-esteem of their followers, adversely affecting the entire working environment. Fourth, toxic leaders value being in control, and they will often go to great lengths to preserve their leadership position.

Category 3
Single Leader Focus

Alpha male leadership: This brand of leadership, discussed at length by Arnold M. Ludwig in his book, *King of the Mountain*, suggests that human beings, like apes and wolves, are hardwired and instinctively driven to have a dominant male be a leader of a social group. Often this leadership brand assigns great weight to physical characteristics as leading predictors of who will emerge as the leader and dominant person in the group. This brand of leadership is gender-oriented in a way that is rejected by many people today. But Ludwig suggests that this brand of leadership is currently displayed in many of the 1,941 heads of nations.

Assigned leadership: This brand refers to leadership based on positions or titles. It is similar to hereditary leadership except that, instead of attaining a leadership position through death (usually of a father), an assigned leader is appointed based on heredity, merit, or other factors. It is very popular in the military. In some cases, assigned leaders are insecure in their positions because they have no popular base. This insecurity often manifests itself as authoritarian, and sometimes even dictatorial, leadership. Accountability is often important to counteract some of the potential negative behavior associated with this type of leadership.

Authentic leadership: This brand, advocated by Kevin Cashman, author of *Leadership from the Inside Out,* defines authentic leadership as the leadership that radiates from the core of a person. He states, "Leadership is authentic self-expression that creates value." Cashman defines five key areas of authentic leadership: (1) knowing oneself authentically; (2) listening authentically; (3) expressing one's self authentically; (4) appreciating authentically; and (5) serving authentically. To be an authentic leader, a person must serve first and lead second. Authentic leaders seek to set an example for all of their followers and for other leaders through their actions and how they approach their leadership responsibilities.

Leadership by example: This brand is adopted by leaders who seek to use their own actions as a guide to their followers. In short, leadership by example implies that leaders should do everything with the same ethical and quality standards that they require of others. There are two parts to this type of leadership: (1) doing what should be done in every situation, and (2) doing it according to high standards of exemplary behavior. Leadership by example can have the positive effect of inspiring followers to have the same goals and commitment as leaders and to adopt their methods and approaches to leadership tasks.

Charismatic leadership: This brand of leadership, discussed in the 1800s by Max Weber and many others, is distinguished from other types of leadership because charismatic leaders inspire people to follow them. Charismatic leaders impress their own visions and goals upon their followers and make their followers see things the way they do. Charismatic leaders radiate self-confidence, lead fearlessly, and know how to communicate their positions and ideas without embarrassment or reservation. Followers often turn to charismatic leaders during times of organizational, corporate, or social turmoil. Charismatic leadership tends to follow the traditional or heroic leadership model. Charismatic leaders lead from the top down, and followers generally do not participate in the decision-making process. One great danger of this brand of leadership is that followers can become blind to what the leader is actually doing and never question what the leader is actually trying to achieve.

Directive leadership: This brand of leadership is the opposite of participative leadership. In times of crisis, people tend to turn to directive leaders, because directive leadership points the way to safety. Directive leaders take charge, make decisions, and expect their decisions to be implemented without question. They are willing to revise goals and provide solutions unilaterally, using the traditional top-down approaches to leading. When the difficult times are past, followers often prefer leaders who are less

160

directive, instead favoring those who seek input before making decisions. Modern history provides numerous examples of directive leadership. For example, democracies tend to reelect directive leaders during times of war. Wartime presidents tend to be more decisive and unilateral than others, and people accept and welcome these traits in times of war or crisis. When the crisis passes, however, the heavy-handed, dictatorial methods of some directive leaders often become unpopular with the voting public. This type of leadership is often replaced by a leader who is more participatory, collaborative, and consultative.

Integrated leadership: This brand of leadership was popularized by Ken Rafferty of Executive Consulting, who argues that integrated leadership involves all aspects of the human condition and creates new ways to get people involved in what they are doing, He says that integrated leadership helps executives understand the power and usefulness of embracing values, trust, participation, learning, creating, and sharing within the work environment. It also involves connecting the various people and departments in an organization with one another to achieve a common purpose decided upon by an organization by involving all of its members in setting the tone and direction for the organization.

Leaders building leaders: This brand or model of leadership has been promoted by Peter Drucker, Jack Welch, and many others. The basic tenet of this brand of leadership is that the primary purpose of a leader is to build up the capabilities of followers so that one can step in and take over should a leader, for any reason, not be able or willing to lead further. The key is that in order for a company to maintain success, the current leaders must continually prepare future leaders. Leaders building leaders is a results-based leadership strategy that promotes future leaders by encouraging "upward" or "trickle-up" leadership and by using 360-degree feedback and other leadership assessment tools. The leaders building leaders brand helps organizations increase their leadership resources, eases transitions, and increases stability.

Leadership at every step: This brand of leadership suggests that leadership is a full-time, 24/7 job and is a lifelong process instead of something that one can do on occasion or as an isolated act during a lifetime. It is an approach used by organizations that believe that leadership can and should occur in every part of an organization and at all times. Leadership at every step implies that all people can lead and have a responsibility to do so.

Postmortem leadership: This brand of leadership describes the influence that strong, heroic leaders can have on their successors and organizations after they leave. This type of leadership can have a profound impact on policy and decision making in the future of many organizations. Postmortem leadership occurs when current leaders try to govern using the formulas and ideas of their predecessor(s) instead of creating their own or following the desires of their followers as they evolve.

Supportive leadership: In *Art of Supportive Leadership*, J. Donald Walters argues that a supportive leader always recognizes that people are very important and not just tools for leaders to use. Supportive leaders are loyal to and supportive of their followers. The classic example of this type of leadership is the general who stays at the front with his troops, despite the dangers to himself. Supportive leaders emphasize having high levels of confidence in and improving the competence of their followers. Supportive leaders are not micromanagers and give their followers substantial room to contribute to leadership decisions and to exhibit leadership behaviors.

Versatile leadership: Robert Kaiser and Robert Kaplan state that versatile leadership consists of a synthesis between balanced leadership and strategic leadership. The versatile leader must balance these leadership traits and approaches at each moment. This type of leadership is dynamic and situationally determined.

Category 4
Interactive Focus

Achievement-oriented leadership: This brand of leadership is one aspect of Robert House's path-goal theory discussed in the text of this book. This type of leader sets high goals and difficult challenges for both the leader and the team. This type of leader also provides encouragement for the members and expresses confidence in the ability of the group to complete the assigned task. Achievement-oriented leaders are ultimately interested in results, but their leadership focuses on more than just the bottom line. By motivating followers, by challenging them, and by giving positive feedback, this leader can promote improved productivity.

Appreciative leadership: This brand of leadership teaches leaders to look for and find the best in people and acknowledge people for the good things they do. It is designed to help facilitate communication between leaders and followers, because the leader actively seeks input from those below him or her. It makes a working environment friendlier by focusing on the positives instead of the negatives. The central idea behind appreciative leadership and its related field, called "appreciative inquiry," is that the leader shows followers that they are appreciated, and he or she tries to work with their strengths whenever possible in order to inspire passion and build self-confidence among them.

Functional leadership or function-centered leadership: This concept, pioneered by Elisabeth Cox and Cynthia House, means that leadership is function-centered rather than person-centered.[1] Leadership is viewed as encompassing critical things to be done, rather than as the characteristics of one person. Function-centered leadership requires that all persons practice leadership by leading in those areas where they have critical responsibilities.

---

1. Elisabeth Cox and Cynthia House, *Functional Leadership: A Model for the Twenty-First Century,* in BUILDING LEADERSHIP BRIDGES 2001 (Univ. of Md., College Park, Md.: Int'l Leadership Ass'n).

Leadership as a process: This brand of leadership makes the distinction between leadership as a solitary act and leadership as a function of the interaction of leaders and followers. Peter Northouse defines leadership as a process during which one individual influences a group of individuals to achieve a common goal.[2] The philosophy behind this brand of leadership views leadership as something that must continually evolve. Leadership is seen as a career or lifelong path. Leadership as a process is a collaborative effort between leaders and followers. It shapes the goals of a group, motivates their behavior toward their attainment of these goals, and defines the culture of the group.

Inclusive leadership: This brand of leadership identifies the fostering of a broad range of interpersonal relationships by the leader as the single most important factor in effective leadership. Inclusive leaders are especially concerned with relationships between them and their followers, customers, investors, suppliers, and the community. They believe that their relationships will lead to sustained growth and development within organizations because they respect their followers and focus on something other than the bottom line. Inclusive leaders act as stewards for their organizations' resources and are willing to share their leadership roles with others. Inclusive leadership views an organization as a network of interpersonal, mutually dependent relationships. Inclusive leaders seek to maximize the potential of the networks. This creates a synergistic effect, because the network, when united in quest of a common goal, produces an even more powerful network. Inclusive leadership is very similar to collaborative, consultative, participatory, and servant leadership in emphasis and practice.

Informed leadership: This brand of leadership involves the creation and support of strong systems to let the leader know what others are thinking and what others know on any particular subject or issue the leader needs to address. The leader who seeks

---

2. Peter Northouse, Leadership: Theory and Practice: Sage Reflections, 3d ed. (Thousand Oaks, Cal., 2004).

to be an informed leader not only creates and pays significant attention to feedback mechanisms, but also creates a culture where every person in the organization or who is a stakeholder feels he or she can speak the truth to power without fear, without sanction, and without any concern that his or her opinion, fact or feedback contribution will be ignored. Informed leaders actually encourage their followers to feel they have a duty to let the leader know what they are thinking or any insight the follower has on a topic. With the possibility of getting daily feedback from thousands of people, informed leaders create systems that will analyze the feedback they are getting, in the form of both quantitative data-like polls and qualitative data expressed in narrative form from their followers. New, sophisticated, analytical approaches to qualitative data yield great insights from large amounts of qualitative information provided to help inform and guide leaders.

Proactive leadership: This brand of leadership is based on the belief that leaders look toward the future and make leadership decisions based on their anticipation of two things: what is going to happen in the future and how their followers are going to react to their ideas, suggestions, decisions, and actions of leadership. This type of leadership requires leaders to understand the future and be able to connect psychologically with their followers. Proactive leaders give feedback and seek 360-degree feedback from those around them. They act decisively and clearly communicate the goals to their followers.

Self-organizing leadership/self-directed teams: Dr. Tomas Hench of the University of Wisconsin, Madison, defines "self-organizing leadership" as "a quality that manifests itself as a relationship between the leader and the led, in the context of a particular challenge, facing a particular group of people, in a particular moment of time." Thus, self-organizing leadership spontaneously manifests itself at any level of an organization in order to meet current challenges. Often, these are communication challenges between and among departments or employees in an organization. Using self-organizing leadership can add significant value to an organization because it helps to capitalize on latent abilities of each member. It also tends to improve work patterns and processes, because people concentrate on building their own future, and lessens resistance to change, because the people themselves are generating and leading the change.

Category 5
Follower Focus

Collaborative leadership: John Gardner, author of *On Leadership,* defines this brand of leadership as one in which leaders seek the strong input of followers in assisting them in making decisions and leading the group. This brand also requires followers to join together and offer their time, assets, and commitment to help formulate key decisions that will address the most difficult issues facing a group. According to John Gardner, collaborative leaders inspire commitment and action by creating visions and working with their followers to solve problems. They lead not from the top down, but as peer problem-solvers who help others without autocratically making decisions. They take responsibility for building extensive community and member involvement and for sustaining hope and participation in their followers. They seek input from all involved parties. They help to keep the group on track by setting realistic, concrete goals and by rewarding the attainment of these goals with positive reinforcement. Collaborative leadership looks at the big picture and at long-term goals and considers the global, complex, and systematic nature of problems.

Consultative leadership: This brand of leadership includes building strong relationships and relies on these relationships for organizations to expand and meet challenges. Consultative leadership allows for the strong participation of followers in the decision-making process. It must be flexible and capable of extending across the leadership/followership border, and actually blur this border. It is designed to deal effectively with problems that are neither clearly defined nor have obvious solutions. Ron Heifetz refers to these kinds of problems as "adaptive problems."

Empowering leadership: This leadership brand is discussed by Peter Block in his book, *The Empowered Manager,* and is very similar to participatory leadership, in which the leader delegates authority to followers, empowering them to make decisions and giving them a direct stake in bringing about change. Theoretically, this reduces the resistance to change and increases the morale of the followers, causing them to work harder, because they are directly involved in leading their organizations.

Entrepreneurial leadership: This brand of leadership instills followers with the confidence to think, behave, and act as entrepreneurs in the interest of their organization. An entrepreneurial leader focuses on encouraging every follower to help create economic value through the deployment of limited resources.

Organizational leadership: This style of leadership, popularized by Theodore White's book *Organizational Man,* stresses allegiance to an organization. It seeks to capitalize on people's desire to be a part of something larger than themselves and urges people to identify themselves as a part of the organization.

Participative leadership: Participative leadership is a type of leadership in which leaders involve others in the decision-making process. Participative leadership is based on the idea that in order to be effective, participative leaders need to encourage their followers to make suggestions and lead the implementation of these suggestions.

Upward/trickle-up leadership/upside-down leadership: Michael Useem, professor at the Wharton School and author of *Leading Up: How to Lead Your Boss So You Both Win,* and Tom Chappell, *Managing Upside Down: Seven Intentions of Value-Centered Leadership,* define upward leadership and trickle-up leadership, in which followers are expected to contribute ideas and help make decisions critical to the future of the organization. Under this definition, leadership originates from the bottom of the corporate pyramid instead of from the higher managerial ranks.

Category 6
Multileader Focus

Distributive leadership: This brand of leadership was made popular by Richard Elmore, professor of educational leadership at Harvard. Distributive leadership stresses the sharing of leadership responsibilities among several people. Distributive leadership is also known as shared leadership, dispersed leadership, fluid leadership, collective leadership, and roving leadership.

Formative leadership: This brand developed by Dr. Ruth Ash and Dr. Maurice Persall from Samford **[au: Samford ok? need location]** University is based upon the idea that many different leaders should work together within a single organization. Law firms often use this type of leadership through management or executive committees. A formative leader must freely share data, information, and knowledge with a team and also facilitate knowledge transfer within the organization to promote wide distribution of leadership tasks throughout the organization.

Category 7
New Challenges Leadership

Connective leadership: This brand of leadership, made popular by Jean Lipman-Blumen's book, *Connective Leadership: Managing in a Changing World,* takes place when leaders reach across borders (corporate, geographical, and cultural) to assist in building communication networks between disparate groups with conflicting needs and goals.

Creative leadership: According to Lyndon Rego from the Center for Creative Leadership, creative leaders seek to anticipate and respond creatively to new situations.

Cross-border leadership: This brand of leadership transcends geographic, cultural, and corporate borders to accomplish a given task. It requires excellent communication skills, because the involved parties often have different (if not conflicting) ideas, expectations, and goals. As the world continues to get smaller (or flatter, as Thomas Friedman suggests), cross-border leadership will become increasingly important.

Category 8
Nontraditional Organizations

"Chaordic" leadership: This brand of leadership was popularized by Dee Hock, founder and CEO emeritus of Visa International, Inc. He coined the term to describe leadership that is both chaotic and orderly. Chaordic leadership differentiates the relationship between superiors/subordinates and between leaders/followers. The former relationship relies upon the coercive power of the supervisor, whereas the latter is a matter of choice for the follower. Chaordic leadership consists of four behaviors, the first three of which should occupy approximately 95 percent of a leader's time: (1) managing one's own character, (2) managing one's peers, (3) managing one's superiors, and (4) managing those below. In this brand of leadership, Dee Hock defies many ethical leadership theorists by proposing that the duty to ensure ethical leadership lies with the followers.

Complexity leadership: This brand of leadership, like quantum leadership, draws on the idea that Newtonian physics is not very applicable to the modern business climate, law firms, corporations, or nonprofit organizations. Complexity leadership encourages spontaneous self-organization and unplanned but sensible improvements in the efficacy of organizations. Complexity leaders do not lead from the top down, but rather expect that their followers will form networks and find ways to lead themselves. This means that goals and production strategies are always being streamlined and ensures that new ideas circulate freely in the organization.

Consultative leadership: This brand of leadership is based upon the belief that many of today's challenges are bigger and more complex than the abilities of any single leader to solve them.

Consultative leaders thus focus on listening, participation, and facilitating a dialogue between themselves and their followers. When done properly, it has a synergistic effect for the entire team and creates better solutions than can be created through a command-and-control or top-down traditional leadership formula. Consultative leadership puts the leader in a role closer to the traditional role of a moderator or facilitator.

Quantum leadership: This brand of leadership borrows its conceptual base from quantum physics and was made popular by Tim Porter-O'Grady's book, *Quantum Leadership: A Textbook of New Leadership.* Although Newtonian physics is dominated by highly structured interactions between objects, quantum theory holds that these interactions are chaotic and unpredictable. Quantum leadership brings this distinction to the world of business and organizational development. Newtonian organizations have the traditional pyramid organizational structure. In Newtonian structures, those on top, the leaders, are expected to control the followers—treating them as tools rather than creative assets. The bureaucratic framework in Newtonian structures is rigid, and multiple layers of approval are required when a person at the bottom of the pyramid makes a suggestion for change or attempts in any way to act as a leader. Newtonian organizations find it difficult to adjust their direction, to innovate, experiment, or adapt in the changing world.

A quantum organization, on the other hand, is one in which all members design and manage the organization's systems and processes. Information flows freely from one area of the organization to the other, not just from the top down. Quantum leadership is based on the idea that anyone within an organization can lead and should develop leadership skills. Quantum leaders help people develop self-managing strategies. Ideally, they teach that organizations are as much about growth and development of the individual members or parts as they are about creating products and delivering services.

Category 9
Results-Oriented Leadership

Results-based leadership: This brand of leadership was popularized by Dave Ulrich, Jack Zenger, and Norman Smallwood in their book, *Results-Based Leadership.* They explain that results-based leadership places a relentless emphasis on outcomes through the following equation: effective leadership = results. One must look to results as the best measure of a leader's ability or aptitude. Results-based leadership focuses on four areas: (1) employee results (i.e., productivity), (2) organizational results, (3) customer-oriented results, and (4) investor results (profits or returns).

Scientific leadership: This brand of leadership focuses on the ability to measure the effects of leaders. The success or failure of a leader who follows the brand or discipline of scientific leadership is determined by how well the people under him or her perform.

Category 10
Leadership Training Brands

Leadership development: This generic category embodies the assumption that leaders are made, not born. Leadership development programs focus on identifying new ways to teach people how to assess and improve their leadership skills. Leadership development courses tend to be based on leadership theories, whereas leadership training is more concerned with fine-tuning technical leadership skills such as speech making, project management, communication, and team-building skills.

Executive development: This aspect or brand of leadership training teaches and develops the skills that high-level managers need. Executive development programs build critical-thinking and decision-making skills necessary to anticipate and meet various challenges.

Leader to leader: This leadership brand asserts that leaders can improve significantly by learning from their peers. According to the Leader to Leader Institute, formerly the Drucker Foundation, bringing leaders into a forum with other leaders helps to facilitate communication and idea generation across the public, private, and social sectors.

Leadership training: This leadership concept is similar to leadership development but focuses on technical aspects of leadership such as project management, public speaking, communication, and team building.

Unnatural leadership: David L. Dotlich and Peter C. Cairo have developed the brand called unnatural leadership, which is learned—hence the name "unnatural." Unnatural leadership promotes the ideas that leaders should think creatively and challenge conventional wisdom, admit when they do not know something, and ask their followers for help. Unnatural leadership embraces these concepts: (1) there are many solutions to a given problem; (2) trust others before they earn it; (3) connect with competitors in symbiotic relationships and avoid having to recreate the wheel; and (4) be willing to give up some control to improve participation.

Category 11
Situational Leadership

Issue leadership: This brand of leadership occurs when a person takes the initial step of organizing a coalition to oppose or support a given issue. The organizers and leaders of the American Civil Liberties Union (ACLU), the National Association for the Advancement of Colored People (NAACP), the Susan B. Anthony List organization, and other single-issue types of organization fall into this category. In general, issue leaders need to be able to focus deeply on one issue and possess good social skills and excellent networking skills.

Leading change: This brand or model of leadership, promoted by John P. Kotter in his book *Leading Change and the Society for the Leadership of Change,* focuses on the intention and ability of a leader to create and execute a vision. People who lead change efforts integrate key program goals, priorities, values, and other factors in a dynamic environment where change both occurs often and is necessary in order to address a problem or situation successfully. Leading change requires the ability to balance change and continuity. Kotter has developed an eight-stage model for implementing change: (1) establish a sense of urgency, (2) create a guiding coalition, (3) develop a vision and strategy, (4) communicate the change and vision, (5) empower a broad base of people to act, (6) generate short-term successes, (7) consolidate gains, and (8) insure that the changes and new approaches are deeply institutionalized into the culture of the organization or society. Leading change requires leaders to be able to predict and understand when followers, and even co-leaders, will resist change in organizations.

Situational leadership: This popular brand of leadership developed and promoted by Hersey and Blanchard refers to a model of leadership that adopts different styles of leading depending on the needs of the situation and the abilities of the leaders and followers in the situation. Ken Blanchard, author of the *One-Minute Manager* series, and Paul Hersey developed the basic model for situational leadership during the 1960s. Situational leadership requires great skill in analyzing a given situation in order to decide which type of leadership style or behavior to use.

Tipping-point leadership: This brand of leadership, first analyzed by Malcolm Gladwell in his book, *Tipping Point,* suggests that for leadership behavior to be effective, leaders should exert a concentrated influence to convince a critical mass of people to adopt an idea or strategy. Tipping-point leaders seek to overcome (1) cognitive hurdles that cause people to resist change, (2) resource hurdles, (3) motivational hurdles, which discourage followers, and (4) political hurdles.

173

Category 12
Team Orientation Leadership

Synergistic leadership: This brand of leadership is based on the notion of having people and organizations work together to create value from the combined efforts that will be far greater than could be created by each of the parts working independently. This intangible factor results in the $1 + 1 = 3$ philosophy. Steven Covey has popularized this type of leadership as Habit #6, Synergize.

Team leadership: This brand of leadership differs from traditional top-down leadership in eight major ways. (1) Instead of one person being solely responsible for the success or failure of an objective, the responsibility is shared by a team of people. (2) Final decisions are made by a group of people and not by an autocratic leader. (3) Power is decentralized, and the structure of authority is deemphasized. (4) The role of the individual is minimized, or at least deemphasized. (5) Task-oriented functions are performed by the group as a whole and not by single leaders. (6) The team itself is responsible for its self-maintenance. (7) Socio-emotional processes and interpersonal interactions are monitored by team leaders. (8) Expressions of feelings and ideas are encouraged and addressed by the team in open meetings. This leadership model can be inefficient and complicated, as compared with the command-and-control model of leadership, especially in large organizations. The expected benefits of team leadership include improving morale, increasing the competence and leadership abilities of all members of the team, and capturing the unique abilities of each member for the good of the entire organization. Team building, an essential component of team leadership, is a leadership strategy involving improving team dynamics, clarifying team goals, identifying roadblocks, overcoming obstacles, and facilitating the achievement of the final goals.

Virtual leadership: This brand of leadership is a field pioneered by NetAge CEO Jessica Lipnack, Jeff Stamps, and Lisa Kimball, CEO of Group Jazz, Inc. It asserts that teams with members in different geographical locations that are managed by a manager who is not geographically located with other team members can be very productive, at significantly less cost, than teams in which everyone is located in the same geographical area using face-to-face meetings and communication. This leadership model relies on information technology to foster and keep track of communications, and places an emphasis on creating team unity. Virtual leaders are in charge of designing the projects and holding the team together, which requires considerable communication, usually by phone, e-mail, Web conferencing, shared documents Web sites, and other collaboration software. The May 2004 issue of the *Harvard Business Review* contains a study about virtual leadership and indicates that it can work very well in today's interconnected, globalized world.

Category 13
Traditional Leadership Brands

Coaching or executive coaching: This brand is a leadership style in which the leader seeks to help people find and explore their own goals and capabilities. This type of leadership encourages two-way communication. Ideally, coaching results in the development of the followers and allows them to become more effective as leaders.

Heroic leadership: This brand of leadership is based on the "great man" theory. Heroic leaders behave as if all the responsibility is on their shoulders and put themselves on a pedestal above their followers. This results in a top-down leadership style that causes followers to become dependent on their leaders.

Institutionalized leadership: This brand of leadership was coined by Elman Service in his 1975 book, *Origins of the State and Civilization: The Process of Cultural Evolution.* Service argues that institutionalized leadership is ingrained both in the legislative foundations of a state and in the functioning of its bureaucratic apparatus. Leadership is therefore fostered by the creation of a detailed institutional framework to allocate decision-making authority.

175

Military leadership: This brand of leadership is organized in a top-down fashion. Military leadership is often marked by a rigid hierarchical structure and a well-defined central authority. A clear definition of values and clear lines of authority must exist for this type of powerful command-and-control leadership to succeed, because often what followers do is a direct function of what the leader says they should do. In times of crisis, military leadership can be especially useful. Followers can clearly identify who is in charge and can be comforted and directed by this person. By establishing exactly how much and what type of authority leaders in each position exert, everyone in the chain of command knows his or her role. However, this style is subject to lack of accountability, because the authority of the position and the authority of the person can be tied very closely and not easily questioned. Often the military leadership brand does not promote significant two-way, reciprocal communication between the leader and the follower.

Muscular leadership: This is a top-down leadership brand that requires strong direction from the leader and strict obedience by followers. This leadership style contrasts with more collaborative, team-oriented approaches to leadership. David Gergen's article "President Bush's Leadership"[3] and his keynote speech to the International Leadership Association in November 2003 in Seattle, Washington,[4] explain how President Bush uses this brand of leadership.

Operational leadership: This brand of leadership, very close to the definition of "management," focuses on the day-to-day challenges facing an organization. In general, this type of leadership is very different from visionary leadership, which focuses its energy on attaining long-term instead of short-term goals.

Powerful leadership: This brand of leadership is espoused by

3. David Gergen, *President Bush's Leadership*, COMPASS: A JOURNAL OF LEADERSHIP, Center for Public Leadership, Harv. Univ. (fall 2003).
4. David Gergen, "Perspectives on Leadership" (Keynote speech; Int'l Leadership Ass'n, Seattle, Wash., November 2003).

Ruth Sherman in *Get Them to See It Your Way, Right Away: How to Persuade Anyone of Anything.* Powerful leaders are able to retain their influence either by building themselves up in the eyes of their followers or by destroying or eliminating their opposition. It also can result in leadership by fear or resentment, which could lower morale and thereby decrease productivity.

Rational leadership: According to Marin Clarke, of the General Management Group at the Cranfield School of Management in England, rational leadership gives priority to traditional and accepted processes of influencing people. Rational leaders tend to prefer formal, face-to-face meetings, and leadership roles are very carefully defined.

Transactional leadership: James Burns popularized this brand of leadership in his book *Leadership,* published in 1976. Transactional leadership motivates followers by appealing to their self-interest. Modern theorists have added to Burns's model, and today there are four types of behavior that can be considered transactional leadership: (1) contingent reward—rewards are given when expectations are met; (2) passive management by exception—correction and punishment are handed out when performance standards are not reached; (3) active management by exception—leaders actively watch work quality and correct followers; and (4) laissez-faire leadership—leaders adopts a hands-off approach to leading.

Category 14
Visionary Leadership

Level five (5) leadership: Jim Collins developed the concept of Level 5 leadership in his book *Good to Great: Why Some Companies Make the Leap . . . and Others Don't.* Collins identified five levels of leadership. Level 1 is provided by very able individuals whose knowledge, experience, and work ethic enables them to lead. Level 2 introduces the concept of teamwork and synergy, stressing that teams can accomplish more than isolated individuals working on similar projects. Level 3 is the leadership demonstrated by the team leader who motivates and encourages a team to succeed. Level 4 resembles Level 3 leadership, but the leader shows more energy and demands more from each team member. Level 5 refers to the leadership given by executives who are personally humble but demand the highest level of performance from their teams. They instill standards and a vision in their followers and use this vision to motivate them. They allow their followers the freedom and responsibility to work together and make their own decisions, while keeping them encouraged and focused on the ultimate goal of the current project. The job of the Level 5 leader is to determine how to best maintain high-level organizational objectives, including cash flow and profitability, and help their followers succeed with all key organizational objectives. Level 5 leaders set an example that they expect their followers to emulate. They sacrifice their own egos in order to help their organizations and accept responsibility for poor performance. According to Collins, Level 5 leadership is the most important factor in taking a company "from good to great."

Loose-tight leadership: This brand of leadership is explained in Christopher Meyer's book, *Relentless Growth: How Silicon Valley Innovation Strategies Can Work in Your Business*. Loose-tight leadership is a style designed to cultivate new ideas on a regular basis. Meyer claims that it "alternates the creation of space for idea generation and free exploration with a deliberate tightening that selects and tests specific ideas for further investment and development." The first stages of innovation should be "loose," and the innovation process should tighten as it progresses. Too much of either loose or tight thinking can harm growth, because looseness can prevent a company from moving forward in a single direction and tightness can strangle creativity. At the heart of this leadership style is the goal of continuous, rapid innovation.

Principle-centered leadership: This brand of leadership is best captured by an excerpt from Stephen R. Covey's book, *Principle-Centered Leadership*. He writes that "if you focus on principles, you empower everyone who understands those principles to act without constant monitoring, evaluating, correcting, or controlling." Principle-centered leadership thus revolves around a set of principles espoused by the leader and accepted by the followers, who may provide some input to the leader regarding these principles. The leader relies upon these principles as the basis for the decisions he or she makes, the style of leadership he or she uses, and as the basis for leading others in its entirety. The principles of security, guidance, wisdom, and power are often key principles that leaders use to guide organizations that adopt this brand of leadership. Principle-centered leadership is similar to the platform-based organizations discussed in this book.

Revolutionary leadership: This brand of leadership is based on the leaders' and followers' perception that significant change is needed in a given community. Revolutionary leaders are willing to take tremendous risks in order to change present conditions and alter the power relationships that currently exist. A basic problem with revolutionary leaders like Pol Pot and others is they often destroy the historic, traditional way of life and all remnants of it, but do not have a coherent strategy to replace this way of life with a better one.

Strategic leadership: According to Randal Heide, onetime president of the Strategic Leadership Forum, strategic leadership compels everyone in an organization to adopt a shared set of goals and a common vision of how to achieve success. Unlike heroic leaders who use fear or personal charisma to inspire followers or results-based leaders who make decisions based only on the bottom line, strategic leaders allow the principles and goals of the organization to guide their leadership decisions and their style of leadership. Strategic leadership ensures that even though leaders come and go, the guidelines for leadership in the organization will remain constant. Dell, Wal-Mart, and Southwest Airlines are all examples of companies that do business according to carefully conceived strategies. Their success does not depend on a specific leader as much as it depends on a constant focus on strategy.

Visionary leadership: This brand of leadership is directed toward meeting long-term, lofty, significant goals. A visionary leader is motivated by a vision of the future. Visionary leaders often can effectively motivate others to work toward this vision. They create huge, but specific, achievable goals, and their leadership style can contain a balance of wisdom, practicality, and motivation, or it can lack an appreciation of how difficult and risky it is to change a currently existing environment.

Category 15
Holistic Follower

Fusion leadership: This brand of leadership has been popularized by Richard L. Daft and Robert H. Lengel in their book, *Fusion Leadership: Unlocking the Subtle Forces That Change People and Organizations*. Fusion leadership brings individuals together to accomplish a goal based on common vision and values. Fusion leaders seek to engage the whole person: the bodies, minds, hearts, and souls of their followers. They support personal growth and creative thinking among followers to facilitate change. Fusion leadership depends on the belief that organizations function as living things. Part of the goal of fusion leadership is to fuse the organization and the individual followers and leaders of the organization so that they grow and change together in similar directions.

Generative leadership: This brand of leadership, taught by Drexel Sprecher and others, does not emphasize influencing other people. Instead, it aims to create an environment in which people continually deepen their understanding of reality, thereby becoming more capable of shaping their own futures. Generative leaders use their abilities to help their followers envision new futures, articulate them, and achieve them.

Transformational leadership: James Burns is given credit for bringing the concept of transformational leadership to the center stage of leadership study and practice. Peter Northouse's book, *Leadership: Theory and Practice,* defines transformational lead-

180

ership as a brand of leadership that makes people want to improve themselves and to be led. Successful transformational leaders are able to assess their followers' needs and show them they are valuable. Four factors are included in transformational leadership: (1) idealized influence—leaders who are trustworthy and are good role models; (2) inspirational motivation—leaders who can motivate people to commit themselves to the ideals of an organization; (3) intellectual stimulation—leaders encourage new ideas and critical thinking; and (4) individual consideration—leaders coach their followers on how to use their strengths and reduce their weaknesses in a constructive way. Transformational leadership emphasizes the needs and strong roles of followers, as well as the reciprocal nature of the leadership/followership relationship.

Category 16
Holistic Leader Focus

Alpha leadership: This brand of leadership, which is distinct from the alpha male brand of leadership, is designed to maximize the effectiveness of leaders while helping them lead more balanced lives. According to Anne Deering, Robert Dilts, and Julian Russell, authors of *Alpha Leadership: Tools for Business Leaders Who Want More from Life,* alpha leadership contains three leadership areas: anticipate, align, and act.

Balanced leadership: This brand of leadership actually has several meanings. It refers to the appropriate balance of numerous personality traits to allow a leader to perform leadership tasks in an integrated manner. Balanced leaders realize that to be effective, they must carefully develop and cultivate their mental, emotional, and physical traits in the proper proportions for a given job. Balanced leadership can also refer to a leadership style that is, in actuality, a combination of several different types of leadership. In certain situations a leader may govern one way, whereas in others he or she may use a different method.

Continuous leadership: This brand of leadership builds on the definition of *leadership at every step*. The idea underlying leadership at every step is that leadership is a full-time activity and every action of a leader must be consistent. Continuous leadership expands on this concept and refers to people who are leaders at all times. Continuous leadership involves acting as a role model for one's followers and living what one teaches.

Enlightened leadership: This type of leadership, according to Ed Oakley and Doug Krug, authors of *Enlightened Leadership: Getting to the Heart of Change,* is represented by the efforts of leaders to make the most out of underutilized talent, expertise, and energy within an organization. Enlightened leadership plays a critical role in mobilizing these latent forces. As Stephen Covey mentions, it works from the inside out. Enlightened leaders first become fully cognizant of their own strengths and weaknesses before evaluating others. Enlightened leaders view problems as opportunities for personal growth, both for followers and for the leader. Enlightened leadership creates an environment of trust and helpfulness, which increases the morale of followers.

Integral leadership: This brand of leadership has been popularized by Ken Wilber. It requires leaders to combine cognitive understanding and technical knowledge with several types of personal consciousness.

Total leadership: This brand of leadership focuses on team development, personal growth, and 360-degree feedback. Dr. Stephen Payne, leadership strategist and pioneer of the total leadership brand, claims that total leaders both achieve better business results and are more fulfilled in their personal lives. Total leadership is designed to integrate work, personal goals, family, and the community.

Wholehearted leadership: This brand of leadership, developed by Dusty Staub and Staub Leadership Consultants, uses the human heart as a model. Because the heart consists of four chambers, wholehearted leadership consists of four main quadrants: competency, integrity, passion, and intimacy. At the core of

182

wholehearted leadership is a purpose, or goal, and to reach this goal, vision and courage are needed. Competency requires being able to understand and deal with the problem at hand and having the commitment to solve it. Integrity involves leading from a moral compass and indicates that ethics play a vital role in wholehearted leadership. Wholehearted leadership is rooted in strong interpersonal relationships that help to transfer the values of leaders to followers. Passion comes from the leader's commitment to achieving certain goals and involves the creation of positive working environments. It also demonstrates the leader's commitment to service. Lastly, intimacy is what makes relationships last, and it allows leaders to show that they care about their followers and the community at large. The wholehearted leader's ability to lead successfully is also based on understanding and meeting the needs of followers.

Leadership Education for Lawyers: Challenges and Promise

Presentation by Herb Rubenstein, Esq.,
to the Association for Continuing
Legal Education Administrators
Denver, Colorado

Introduction

The legal profession and law schools in particular are currently very resistant to introducing "leadership development education" into law school and CLE curricula. A new course called "Leadership in the Public Sector" has been instituted at Harvard University as an elective for law students. My research shows that with the exception of "Leadership for Lawyers" in Cincinnati, no state bar association has approved of a CLE course on "leadership or leadership development" or "leadership theory and practice" for CLE credit in the United States.

I come before you today hoping to be proven wrong in my last assertion. And, if I am not wrong, I hope to convince you today why leadership education is very important to lawyers, why I believe courses in leadership could be very popular programs for CLE, and why the profession could be greatly improved by the creation of leadership development courses for lawyers. Since I only have a short time with you today, I will only touch on a few key points of my argument. Ultimately, only good courses and good marketing will determine if there is demand for these courses and if they are useful to lawyers in their everyday lives as professionals leading their clients, their client organizations and litigation situations.

For Lawyers by Lawyers

I accept from the outset that if a course on leadership is going to be taught to lawyers, it first must be taught by lawyers. Second, it must be based on a rigorous review of the current leadership literature and knowledge base in the field of leadership. Lawyers have a right to demand excellence when a new course is being sold to them, especially one that does not add to the ever-growing demand for technical, law-related courses that help lawyers keep up with the increasingly complex field of law.

Third, any course on leadership must be practical and must be grounded, at least in part, in the tradition of the case method. Since the leadership literature is usually not grounded in the case method, leadership development courses must be developed to use fact patterns that lawyers face with great regularity. Fourth, leadership development courses must also intersperse leadership theory, skills, knowledge and practices so that lawyers in a three-hour format can get a taste of how to improve their own leadership capabilities.

The Why Behind the Course

Lawyers are called upon to be leaders every day. Sole practitioners who serve on boards due to their sense of duty and their desire to market their services in an honorable way go into these governance situations without proper leadership training. Leaders of large law firms must go to Harvard's MBA program to take a one-week course called, "Managing the Professional Service Organization." And one former president of the D.C. Bar Association whom I met at the end of his tenure told me that he certainly could have benefited from a strong leadership development course in his job as bar president.

Today, the legal profession's reputation in the community as a whole is not a source of great pride to the profession. Leadership education could help support lawyers becoming better leaders, and, I believe, such a course could help lawyers earn a better reputation in the world at large.

The Course at Harvard Law School (HLS)

From my recent interview with Professor Phillip Heymann and my review of the HLS Catalogue, I learned the following information about the leadership course for law students at Harvard. The following is directly quoted from the catalogue:

Leadership in the Public Sector
Professor Phillip B. Heymann
3 classroom credits 41790-31 Spring

Attempting to combine knowledge about personal, organizational, and political relationships through integrating concepts such as 'organizational strategy,' the course will develop a descriptive and normative picture of the job and responsibility of an elected or an appointed government official. The examples will emphasize lawyers in governmental or political roles. The methodology relies extensively on case studies of people and events, such as: David Kessler addressing smoking at the Food and Drug Administration; Barry McCaffrey as drug czar; Jim Woolsey dealing with spying by Aldrich Ames at the CIA; Governor Hunt and Senator Helms designing political campaigns; or Bill Bratton trying to make-over the N.Y.P.D. The object of the course is to increase the sophistication of students about the operations and interaction of government and politics.

End of catalogue section.

Phil Heymann also stated that he did not know of any other course on leadership for law students or CLE and strongly believes that the profession would be well served to begin to have leadership development courses, just as MBA and other graduate programs have them as required courses for a degree.

The CLE Leadership Course I Envision

In the first stage of the development of this leadership course, I envision a course that describes the 10 leadership theories, describes the 80+ current brands of leadership on the market, and identifies and explains the 50+ basic leadership behaviors generally accepted as the standards by which leaders must operate.

By laying out the 10 modern leadership theories, in an evolutionary framework (each latter one builds on the former), students will gain important, practical insights regarding how the current evolution in what we call "leadership" can improve our workplaces, productivity, employee retention, profits, professionalism, decision making, problem solving, and reduce strife inside the workplace. Peter Northouse, in the third edition of *Leadership Theory and Practice* (Sage, 2003), has given us a useful framework or lens to look at leadership theories. Each of the nine basic theories of leadership he has identified, plus my own theory of "Leaders of Leaders," is summarized below.

1. *The Trait Theory:* People with certain physical, mental, personality-based and emotional traits are more likely, if not destined, to be leaders.
2. *The Style Approach:* Leadership is a function of the style of behavior a person brings to a situation. Typical styles of leadership activity include: Team Management, Authority-Compliance; Country Club Management and Impoverished Management.
3. *The Situational Approach:* Leaders must "read" a situation and determine what combination of supportive and directive behaviors is appropriate. Such behaviors may be characterized as delegating (low supportive, low directive); supporting (high supportive and low directive);

188

coaching (high supportive and high directive) and directing (low supportive and high directive). This leadership theory suggests that leaders adapt their styles based on understanding the full content and context of the situation they are in, their role, the goals of the situation and their assessment of what is needed.

4. ***The Contingency Theory:*** Leadership situations can be characterized into three distinct groupings: 1) leader-member relations; 2) task structure; and 3) position power. Contingency theory analyzes how the success of certain styles of leadership are contingent on the circumstances in which they are used. This theory suggests that the situation will have a strong impact on the leader and leadership style which will be effective in that situation.

5. ***Path-Goal Theory:*** This is the motivational theory of leadership. This theory suggests that a major goal of leadership is to stimulate performance and satisfaction among those led by the leader. The classic behaviors of the leader under this theory are: 1) identify goals and secure "buy in," support, enthusiasm, ownership of these goals by subordinates; 2) identify all key obstacles to achieving the goals; 3) assure proper training and resources for subordinates in their effort to achieve these goals; 4) organize and direct the actions of the subordinates in their effort to achieve goals; 5) monitor all activity and guide any changes in strategy, resources and actions necessary to achieve goals; 6) lead the actions to achieve the goals; 7) acknowledge and reward subordinates for contributions in the effort to achieve the goals; 8) set new goals and repeat process.

6. ***Leader-Member Exchange Theory:*** This theory suggests that leadership is a function of a relationship where followers give to a leader leadership status and responsibilities and leaders accept that status, perform leadership acts which the followers accept, and the relationship between the leader and followers is one of partnership rather than control. Power is equally shared

189

by members with the leader and the leader's ability and authority to lead is always a function of the support he or she has from the members.

7. ***Transformational Leadership:*** Leadership is a process that changes and transforms individuals and groups. It is a dynamic process which includes assessing the follower's needs and motives and seeking the input of the followers at each critical stage in the leadership process. Transformational leadership presupposes that the goal of the leader is to promote change and improvement for the betterment and with the assistance of the followers.

8. ***Team Leadership:*** This theory assumes that all leaders are leaders of teams and the major functions of a leader are 1) to help the group determine which goals and tasks it wants to achieve; 2) help create enabling processes and direct the group so that it performs the tasks and achieves the goals; 3) keep the group supplied with the right resources, training and supplies; 4) set standards for behavior, success and ethics; 4) diagnose and remedy group deficiencies; 5) forecast impending environmental changes to help steer the group; 6) help maintain and defend the group by organizing it and insuring its proper internal functioning.

9. ***Psychodynamic Approach:*** This theory suggests that successful leaders must understand their own psychological makeup and the psychological makeup of those they lead. Leaders in this theory are those who understand the 1) "family of origin" impact on a person's attitude, potential, behaviors and expected responses to leadership; 2) the level of maturity of followers and its impact on their responses to leadership actions; 3) the desire and motivational keys to the subordinates; 4) the meaning and interpretation of language, behavior, symbols and expected understanding of situations by subordinates; 5) the proper balance of dependence and independence appropriate for a given group of followers; 6) the proper psychological

relationship between the leader and subordinates; and 7) the understanding of the psychodynamic interplay between the leader and subordinates and between and among leaders as well as subordinates. Leaders must be able to incorporate these dimensions in creating their leadership style and activities so they will succeed.

10. ***Leaders of Leaders:*** This theory of leadership suggests that the job of a leader of followers is completely different from that of a job of a leader of leaders. Leaders of followers are mainly "problem solvers." Leaders of leaders are "platform setters" who create a platform that guides the environment for the followers so that they can act within this environment as leaders themselves, solve their own "problems," and make excellent decisions consistent with the platform that the leader of leaders sets. In addition, the leaders of leaders concept incorporates the idea that the platform set by the leader of leaders will improve over time as the followers and other leaders will be encouraged to test the platform out in the real world, find deficiencies and report proposed improvements for the platform to the leader of leaders. The major role of the leader of leaders is to create this platform and not to make decisions in particular situations. This job is delegated to the leaders whom the leader of leaders leads.

From Theory to Brands

It is axiomatic that "theory will only get you so far." In the commercial or product "space," we go from idea/theory to "brand" as the next conceptual link to the customer's mind and wallet. Not surprisingly, we do the same in the academic or intellectual space. Today, we have over 80 brands of leadership currently available from vendors, books, trainers and "leadership gurus" throughout the United States and the world. Each brand has its marketing program, course materials, tapes, books, CDs and speakers, and each attempts to corner one niche market of the leadership industry by differentiating itself from all of the oth-

191

ers. Below is an exhausting, but not exhaustive, list of leadership brands on the market today.

Assigned Leadership. Connective Leadership. Balanced Leadership. Connected Leadership. Muscular Leadership. Toxic Leadership. Fusion Leadership. Complexity Leadership. Character-Based Leadership. Emergent Leadership. Directive Leadership. Participative Leadership. Ethical Leadership. Principled Leadership. Team Leadership. Achievement-Oriented Leadership. Supportive Leadership. Charismatic Leadership. Wholehearted Leadership. Level 5 Leadership. Authentic Leadership. Leadership Development. Leadership Training. Executive Development. Team Building. Coaching. Situational Leadership. Principle-Centered Leadership. Values-Centered Leadership. Inclusive Leadership. Servant Leadership. Transactional Leadership. Transformational Leadership. Total Leadership. Trustee Leadership. Leadership Identity. Enlightened Leadership. Leadership at Every Step. Leading Change. Values-Based Leadership. Continuous Leadership. Rational Leadership. Visionary Leadership. Strategic Leadership. Contributory Leadership. Virtual Leadership. Leadership by Example. Integrated Leadership. Institutionalized Leadership. Collaborative Leadership. Appreciative Leadership. Leadership as a Process. Proactive Leadership. Generative Leadership. Revolutionary Leadership. Total Leadership. Unnatural Leadership. Empowering Leadership. Organizational Leadership. Operational Leadership. Innovative Leadership. Creative Leadership. Synergistic Leadership. Entrepreneurial Leadership. Steward Leadership. Military Leadership. Inspired Leadership. Leaders Building Leaders. Leading Upward. Tomorrow Leader. Quantum Leadership. Alpha Leadership. Lead by Design. Results-Based Leadership. Trickle-Up Leadership. Leaders to Leaders. Formative Leadership. Distributive Leadership. Integral Leadership. Cross-Border Leadership. Invisible Leadership. Social Leadership.

From Brand to Behavior

Every creator of an idea or product knows that "brand" is only the lubricant in the sales process. There must, at some point, be some "beef" in the burger, or "tofu" in the dish, to generate constant, profitable sales and an increase in the value of the brand. Below are sets of leadership behaviors classified similarly to the way we classify a genus, species and classes of birds or mammals. A list of prominently acknowledged sets of successful leadership behaviors is presented below. The leadership course that I envision would, at least, educate the lawyer on these types of behaviors that are expected of leaders today.

Checklist 1: People Management

1.1 Clearly communicates expectations

1.2 Recognizes, acknowledges and rewards achievement

1.3 Inspires others and serves as a catalyst for others to perform in ways they would not undertake without the leader's support and direction

1.4 Puts the right people in the right positions at the right time with the right resources and the right job description

1.5 Secures alignment on what is the right direction for the organization

1.6 Persuades/Encourages people in the organization to achieve the desired results for the organization

1.7 Makes sure not to burn out people in the organization, looking out for their well-being as well as the well-being of the organization

1.8 Identifies weak signals that suggest impending conflict and deals with the sources of conflict effectively

1.9 Holds people accountable

1.10 Encourages the human capital development of every person in the organization and allocates sufficient resources to this endeavor

1.11 Correctly evaluates the actual performance and the potential of each person in the organization

1.12 Encourages people in the organization to stand up for and express their beliefs

1.13   Creates a non-fear-based environment where every person in the organization can speak the truth as he or she sees it without concern for retaliation

1.14   Able to empathize with those he or she leads

Checklist 2: Strategic Management

2.1   Flexible when necessary to adapt to changing circumstances

2.2   Sets, with input from others including all stakeholders, the long-term direction for the organization

2.3   Understands the competitive environment, social trends, competitors, customers and all stakeholders

2.4   Correctly analyzes the risks of all decisions

2.5   Correctly analyzes the returns of all decisions

2.6   Has the ability to focus without losing breadth in his or her ability to see at the outer edges, gathering worthwhile information that others miss or fail to see as significant

2.7   Understands the strengths and weaknesses of the organization and how to exploit the strengths and address the weaknesses successfully

2.8   Can develop and implement strategies to improve the strengths and to combat the weaknesses of the organization

2.9   Can identify appropriate partners, strategic alliances and outside resources to tap into to help further the organization's goals

2.10   Can articulate the values of the organization and develop strategies consistent with the core values

2.11   Demonstrates a strong commitment to diversity and change, improvement

2.12   Demonstrates a strong commitment to creating and sustaining a learning organization (Learning is the foundation for all sustainable change.).

Checklist 3: Personal Characteristics

3.1 Lives with honesty and integrity

3.2 Selects people for his or her team who are honest and have high integrity

3.3 Will, passion and desire to succeed

3.4 Willingness to shoulder the responsibility for success (without being a "thunder taker") and failure (without casting blame)

3.5 Innovative and open to new ideas

3.6 Not willing to accept the ways things are as they can always be improved; never satisfied completely with the status quo

3.7 Smart, intelligent, emotionally strong

3.8 Confident without being arrogant

3.9 Able negotiator

3.10 Willing to be patient

3.11 Decisive when necessary

3.12 Able to think analytically

3.13 Quick learner

3.14 Respectful to all

3.15 Perceptive and sensitive to the needs of others

3.16 Diligent, disciplined and has strong perseverance capabilities

3.17 Comfortable with ambiguity

3.18 Willing to be original

3.19 Informed risk-taker

Checklist 4: Process Management

4.1 Able to manage change

4.2 Promotes innovation

4.3 Able to secure resources

4.4 Able to allocate resources

4.5 Great problem-solver

4.6 Able to anticipate crises

4.7 Able to handle crisis when it explodes

4.8 Can create and manage budgets

4.9   Can create and manage time lines, work plans
4.10   Great project management skills
4.11   Can translate long-term vision into step-by-step plan
4.12   Able to measure results
4.13   Knows when a process is not working
4.14   Willing to redesign processes as often as necessary

The Second Generation Course

The second generation course, which would be four hours of CLE, and would be offered in the second year that leadership development courses would be offered, would be similar to the original course and would include a leadership diagnostic instrument that each person taking the course would take in advance (walk-ins would take it during the first break, and it could be scored electronically during the second hour of the course). This course would include all of the material from the first course, updated from what is learned teaching the course for one full year, plus 45 minutes of explanation of the leadership diagnostic results in a general framework.

Each person attending the course would receive a confidential leadership "profile" or report, and this additional service could help individual lawyers understand their own personal strengths and weaknesses as leaders.

There are hundreds of leadership diagnostic tools that are available, and research needs to be undertaken to determine the best tool for the legal profession. Also, these tools are very expensive ($195 and up) if very few people are taking them, but can cost as little as $20 when thousands of people are using the same instrument. Thus, after a first year of leadership development courses being offered around the country, one could predict with some accuracy the number of people expected to take the course and could negotiate a very favorable rate for a leadership diagnostic tool. In addition, it would give the course creators and teachers some time to study the leadership diagnostic instruments so as to select the one that is the most relevant to the legal profession.

Various Formats

Leadership courses for lawyers can be offered in a stand-up format with a 40-page booklet or notebook of key information to guide the student. This typical CLE format could be taught with up to 200 people in the room, or even more. In addition, the material can be delivered in a completely electronic form. E-learning systems are available that can ensure that the course taker has spent three or four hours on the material and can be laced with questions to ensure that the person taking the course at least answers the questions. This will ensure that people earn the credit they get for the course.

The course can also be taught with a 1.0-hour ethics component. There is a strong movement to create a "theory of ethical leadership" that could easily comprise 45 minutes to one hour of time worthy of 1.0 hours credit for ethics. In addition, the course could be offered in the one-hour and two-hour formats used by many states, or even expanded to eight hours.

Conclusion

The field of leadership development for the entire legal profession is wide open. It is no accident that Harvard has decided to take the lead in this area, since the school teaches its students, first and foremost, that they will be the leaders of society in the future.

I think the time is right for such a course to catch fire in the legal profession, especially at the CLE level. I welcome your comments and, hopefully, your partnership in making this a reality in the very near future.

Bibliography

Albert, Ethel M., Theodore C. Denise, and Sheldon P. Peterfruend. *Great Traditions in Ethics*. Belmont, Cal.: Wadsworth Publishing Company, 1988.

American Bar Association. *Annotated Model Rules of Professional Conduct*, 5th ed. Chicago: ABA Center for Professional Responsibility, 2002.

Aquinas, Thomas. *On Law, Morality, and Politics*. Indianapolis: Hackett Publishing Co., 1988.

Aristotle. *Nicomachean Ethics,* http://encarta.msn.com/encyclopedia_761553008/Natural Law_(ethics).html

Aune, Bruce. *Kant's Theory of Morals.* Princeton: Princeton University Press, 1979.

Austin, John. *Lectures on Jurisprudence and the Philosophy of Positive Law.* St. Clair Shores, Mich.: Scholarly Press, 1977.

Bennis, Warren. *On Becoming a Leader*. Cambridge: Perseus Books Group, 2003.

Bennis, Warren, and Joan Goldsmith. *Learning to Lead. A Workbook on Becoming a Leader*, 3d ed. Cambridge: Basic Books, 2003.

Blackstone, William. *Commentaries on the Law of England.* Chicago: University of Chicago Press, 1979.

Blanchard, Kenneth, and Spencer Johnson. *The One Minute Manager*. New York: William Morrow Publishers, 1982.

Block, Peter. *The Empowered Manager: Positive Political Skills at Work.* San Francisco: Jossey-Bass, 1987.

Bloom, Michael A. "Lawyers and Alcoholism: Is It Time for a New Approach?" *Temple Law Review* 61 (1988): 1409.

Burns, James M. *Leadership.* New York: Harper and Row, 1978.

Cardozo, Benjamin. *Cardozo: The Growth of Law.* New Haven: Yale University Press, 1924.

Cardozo, Benjamin. Cardozo. *Cardozo: The Nature of the Judicial Process.* New Haven: Yale University Press, 1924.

Cashman, Kevin. *Leadership From the Inside Out.* Provo, Utah: Executive Excellence Publishing, 1998.

"The Changing Role of the Jury in the Nineteenth Century," 74 *Yale L. J.* (1964).

Chappell, Tom. *Managing Upside Down: Seven Intentions of Value-Centered Leadership.* New York: William Morrow Publishers, 1999.

Ciulla, Joanne B. *Ethics, The Heart of Leadership,* 2d ed. New York: Praeger, 2004.

Ciulla, Joanne B. *The Ethics of Leadership.* London: Wadsworth Books, 2003.

Clifford, Robert. "Opening Statement: Confronting Our Critics." *Litigation* 28, no. 2. Chicago: American Bar Association, 2001.

Collins, James C., and Jerry I. Porras. *Built to Last.* New York: Harper Business, 1995.

Collins, James. *Good to Great: Why Some Companies Make the Leap . . . And Others Don't.* New York: HarperCollins, 2001.

Confucius, *Analects* (2004). http://www.hm.tyg.jp/~acmuller/contao/analects.htm.

Conrad, Clay S. *Jury Nullification, The Evolution of a Doctrine.* Carolina Academic Press, 1998.

Constitution of the United States, www.law.cornell.edu/ constitution/constitution.overview.html.

Covey, Stephen. *The Seven Habits of Highly Effective People.* New York: Simon & Schuster, 1989.

Covey, Stephen. *Principle-Centered Leadership.* New York: Fireside-Simon & Schuster, 1990.

Cox, Elisabeth, and Cynthia House. "Functional Leadership: A Model for the Twenty-First Century." *Building Leadership Bridges 2001.* College Park, Md.: International Leadership Association, 2001.

Daicoff, Susan Swaim. *Lawyer Know Thyself: A Psychological Analysis of Personality Strengths and Weaknesses.* Washington, D.C.: American Psychological Association, 2004.

Dau-Schmidt, Ken, and Kaushik Mukhopdhaya. "The Fruits of Our Labors: An Empirical Study of the Distribution of Income and Job Satisfaction Over the Legal Profession." 49 *Journal of Legal Education* 342, 1999.

Drachman, Virginia G. *Women Lawyers and the Origins of Professional Identity in America: The Letters of the Equity Club, 1887 to 1890.* Ann Arbor: University of Michigan Press, 1993.

Daft, Richard L., and Robert H. Lengel. *Fusion Leadership: Unlocking the Subtle Forces That Change People and Organizations.* San Francisco: Barrett Koehler, 1998.

Deering, Anne, Robert Dilts, and Julian Russell. *Alpha Leadership: Tools for Business Leaders Who Want More From Life.* San Francisco: Jossey-Bass, 2002.

Downs, Larry. "The Killer App." *Harvard Business Review.* December, 2004.

Ellis, Joseph J. *Founding Brothers*. New York: Vintage Books, 2002.

Coughlin, Linda, Ellen Wingard, Keith Hollihan, eds. *Enlightened Power: How Women are Transforming the Practice of Leadership*. San Francisco: Jossey-Bass, 2005.

Fels, Anna. *Necessary Dreams: Ambition in Changing Women's Lives*. Boston: Harvard Business Books, 2004.

Fuller, Lon L. *The Morality of Law*. New Haven: Yale University Press, 1964.

Fuchs Epstein, Cynthia. *Women in Law*. New York: Basic Books, 1981.

Gardner, John W. *On Leadership*. New York: The Free Press, 1990.

Gardner, Howard. *Leading Minds: An Anatomy of Leadership*. New York: Harper Collins, 1995.

Gergen, David. "President Bush's Leadership." *Compass: A Journal of Leadership*. Cambridge: Center for Public Leadership, Harvard University, 2003.

Gergen, David. "Perspectives on Leadership." Seattle: Keynote Address, International Leadership Association, 2003.

Gladwell, Malcolm. *The Tipping Point: How Little Things Can Make a Great Difference*. New York: Little, Brown & Company, 2000.

Granfield, Robert. "Do Law Students Abandon Their Ideals? The Crisis of Idealism in the Age of Affluence." *Legal Studies Forum*, Vol. XVIII, No. 1, 1994.

Greenleaf, Robert. *Servant Leadership: A Journey into the Nature of Legitimate Power of Greatness*. Mahwah, N.J.: Paulist Press, 1977.

Grzelakowski, Moe. *Mother Leads Best: 50 Women Who Are Changing the Way Organizations Define Leadership*. Chicago: Dearborn Trade, 2005.

Harrington, Mona. *Women Lawyers, Rewriting the Rules.* New York: Penguin Group, 1995.

House, R.J., and T.R. Mitchell. "Path-Goal Theory of Leadership." *Journal of Contemporary Business* 3 (1974): 81-97.

Kabacoff, Robert I. *Gender and Leadership in the Corporate Boardroom.* Portland, Me.: Management Research Group. www.mrg.com/Publications/articles/APA2000.pdf..

Klenke, Karin. *Women and Leadership. A Contextual Perspective.* New York: Springer Publishers, 1996.

Kotter, John P. *Leading Change.* Boston: Harvard Business School Press, 1996.

Kouzes, James, and Barry Z. Posner. *The Leadership Challenge: How to Get Extraordinary Things Done in Organizations,* 3d ed. San Francisco: Jossey-Bass, 2002.

Lavan, Helen. "Dissatisfied Attorneys Have Plenty of Options." www.careerjournal.com.

Linowitz, Sol. M., and Martin Mayer. *The Betrayed Profession: Lawyering at the End of the Twentieth Century.* Baltimore: Johns Hopkins University Press, 2000.

Lipman-Blumen, Jean. *The Allure of Toxic Leaders: Why We Follow Destructive Bosses.* Oxford: Oxford University Press, 2004.

Lipman-Blumen, Jean. *Connective Leadership: Managing in a Changing World.* Oxford: Oxford University Press, 1996.

Ludwig, Arnold M. *King of the Mountain.* Lexington: University of Kentucky Press, 2004.

Maccoby, Michael. *The Productive Narcissist: The Promise and Peril of Visionary Leaders.* New York: Broadway Books, 2003.

MacIntyre, Alasdair. *A Short History of Ethics.* New York: Macmillan Company, 1968.

Mason, Alpheus Thomas. *Brandeis: A Free Man's Life.* New York: Viking Press, 1946.

Meyer, Christopher. *Relentless Growth: How Silicon Valley Innovation Strategies Can Work in Your Business.* New York: Free Press, 1998.

Milgram, Stanley. "Behavioral Study of Obedience." 67 *J. Abnormal & Soc. Psychol.* 371, 1963.

Miller, William Lee. *Lincoln's Virtues, an Ethical Biography.* New York: Alfred A. Knopf, 2002.

Morello, Karen Berger. *The Invisible Bar: The Woman Lawyer in America: 1638 to the Present.* New York: Random House, 1986.

Munsey, Brenda. *Moral Development, Moral Education and Kohlberg.* Birmingham, Ala.: Religion Education Press, 2004.

National Conference on Public Trust and Confidence in the Judicial System, http:aja.ncsc.dni.us/courtrv/review.html (1999).

Nischwitz, Jeffrey L. *Think Again: Innovative Approaches to the Business of Law.* Chicago: ABA, Law Practice Management Section, 2007.

Northouse, Peter G. *Leadership Theory and Practice,* 2d ed. and 3d ed. Thousand Oaks, Calif.: Sage Publications, 2001, 2004.

Oakley, Ed, and Doug Krug. *Enlightened Leadership: Getting to the Heart of Change.* New York: Simon & Schuster, 1994.

O'Brien, William J. *The Soul of Corporate Leadership: Guidelines for Value-Centered Governance.* Waltham, Mass.: Pegasus Books, 1998.

O'Toole, James. *The Executive's Compass.* Oxford: Oxford University Press, 1993.

Peskowitz, Miriam. *The Truth Behind the Mommy Wars, Who Decides Who Makes a Good Mother.* Emeryville, Cal.: Seal Press, 2005.

Porter O'Grady, Tim. *Quantum Leadership: A Textbook of New Leadership.* Sudbury, Mass.: Jones & Bartlett Publishers, 2003.

Power, F. Clark, Ann Higgins, and Lawrence Kohlberg. *Lawrence Kohlberg's Approach to Moral Education.* New York: Columbia University Press, 1989.

Rost, Joseph. *Leadership for the 21st Century.* New York: Praeger, 1991.

Rubenstein, Herb, and Tony Grundy. *Breakthrough, Inc.: High Growth Strategies for Entrepreneurial Organizations.* London: Prentice Hall/Financial Times, 1999.

Ruderman, Maria, and Patricia Ohlott. *Standing at the Crossroads: Next Steps for High-Achieving Women.* San Francisco: Jossey-Bass, 2002.

Seligman, Martin E.P., Paul R. Verkuil, and Terry H. Kang. "Why Lawyers Are Unhappy." *Cardozo Law Review* 23 (2001): 33

Service, Elman. *Origins of the State and Civilization: The Process of Cultural Evolution.* New York: W.W. Norton., 1975.

Sherman, Ruth. *Get Them to See It Your Way, Right Away: How to Persuade Anyone of Anything.* New York: McGraw Hill, 2004.

Silvestra, Marissa. *Women in Charge, Policing Gender and Leadership.* Devon, England: Willan, 2003.

Staub, Robert E. *The Heart of Leadership: 12 Practices of Courageous Leaders.* Greensboro, N.C.: Staub Leadership Publishing, 2002.

Stefancic, Jean, and Richard Delgado. *How Lawyers Lose Their Way: A Profession Fails Its Creative Minds.* Durham: Duke University Press, 2005.

"The Debate: Do Men and Women Have Different Leadership Styles? The Case for," by Susan Vinnicombe, Director of the Centre for Developing Women Business Leaders, and "The Case Against," by Andrew Kakabadse, Professor of International Management Development. *Management Focus.* Issue 12, Summer 1999, Cranfield School of Management, England.

Thoreau, Henry David. *Civil Disobedience.* Cambridge: Riverside Press, 1849.

Ulrich, Dave, Jack Zenger, and Norman Smallwood. *Results-Based Leadership: How Leaders Build the Business and Improve the Bottom Line.* Boston: Harvard Business School Press, 1999.

Universal Declaration of Human Rights (1948). http://www.un.org/Overview/rights.html.

Useem, Michael. *Leading Up: How to Lead Your Boss So You Both Win.* New York: Crown Books, 2001.

Walters, J. Donald. *Art of Supportive Leadership: A Practical Handbook for People in Positions of Responsibility*, 2d ed. Nevada City, Cal.: Crystal Clarity Publishers, 1987.

Warren, Roger K. "Public Trust and Procedural Justice." *Court Review*, Fall 2000.

Wheatley, Meg. *Leadership and the New Science: Learning About Organizations from an Orderly Universe.* San Francisco: Barrett-Koehler, 1992.

Index

About the Author

Herb Rubenstein is a Phi Beta Kappa graduate of Washington and Lee University. He received a Rotary Foundation Ambassadorial Scholarship to attend The University of Bristol in England, where he received a graduate diploma in the social sciences. He received his masters of public affairs degree from the Lyndon Baines Johnson School of Public Affairs of the University of Texas at Austin. He received his law degree from Georgetown University in 1982.

He worked at the National Academy of Sciences, the American Institutes for Research, and the U.S. Department of Health and Human Services prior to beginning his private practice of law. He has been a member of the board of directors of the International Leadership Association and was a founding member of the Association of Professional Futurists.

Herb serves as the chief operating officer of the International Center for Appropriate and Sustainable Technology after serving as the development director for the Autism Society of Colorado. In addition to the first and second editions of *Leadership for Lawyers,* he is author of *Breakthrough, Inc: High Growth Strategies for Entrepreneurial Organizations* and more than 100 articles on leadership, strategic planning, organizational development, and law-related topics. He has taught strategic planning, leadership, and entrepreneurship as an adjunct professor at five universities. He also has been a candidate for Congress in the Seventh Congressional District of Colorado. Herb is married and has two children.